The
Hunter's
Cookbook

The Hunter's Cookbook

by
Betty Melville

Heidelberg Publishers

3707 Kerbey Lane   Austin, Texas 78731

Standard Book Number: 0-913206-00-8
Library of Congress Catalog Card Number: 72-89047
Printed in the United States of America

Photographic conversions made from half-tones
provided by the Texas Parks and Wildlife.

Design by Larry Smitherman

To my husband, who furnished the
materials and inspiration for this book.

Contents

Intro-
duction

Wild game cookery is a culinary challenge which should be, and can be, met with an equal degree of success and pleasure. For more than twenty-five years I have prepared for my family and friends innumerable meals from the game animals they brought home from hunting trips in the mountains and plains of New Mexico and neighboring states. When I first began cooking wild game there were few cookbooks on the subject, and because the game I had to prepare was frequently of an uncommon variety, I was soon faced with the necessity of experimenting with the domestic meat recipes available to me. I learned the peculiarities of the many varieties of wild game meats, and found that often their differences from domestic meats proved them to be superior in both flavor and nutrition.

I realize that in many cases it falls to the hunter to prepare his own game for the table. Because of this, and because the quality of the completed meal depends greatly on the proper treatment of the meat before it reaches the kitchen, I have included sections on field dressing, processing, and preserving wild game along with these recipes. These sections are important. It is a shame and a waste that so many beautiful animals are ruined due to improper field preparation, poor knowledge of cooking, and lack of respect for the animal itself.

In compiling this book, it is my hope that much enjoyment and feeling of accomplishment may be passed on to the wives of proud hunters, wherever they may be. If my recipes help you to be a better cook, I will be most pleased.

Betty Melville

Field Dressing

Large Game

Freshly killed game requires more prompt attention to bleeding, chilling, and dressing than do domestic animals. Body heat encourages bacterial decay, so it is important to remove the intestines and to allow the carcass to cool as soon as possible. Virtually all big game animals (deer, elk, sheep, antelope, buffalo) are field dressed in a similar manner.

It is important to have a strong-bladed knife for dressing large game because you must cut cartilages and bones rather quickly and a small knife is not sufficient. Lay the animal on its back and prop it in that position by placing stones or logs on either side of it. It is not necessary to cut the throat for bleeding because the animal will be bled better and faster during the field dressing. The scent, or musk, glands should be removed first, being careful that none of the odor is allowed to contaminate other parts of the carcass. These glands are located inside the hind legs, under the forelegs, or on the back of the spine near the rump. If the animal is male the genitals should be removed next.

Starting between the hind legs, cut all the way down to the pelvic bone. Then turn the knife blade upward and cut all the way up through the breast bone using your free hand to hold the skin away from the intestines so they will not be punctured by the knife blade. Cut up the neck as far as possible, and then sever the windpipe. Grasping the windpipe with both hands, pull hard downward. This should remove the intestines all the way down to the mid-section. Roll the carcass over on one side and cut the thin layer of flesh holding the entrails to the ribs. Next roll the carcass on the other side and do the same. Then, using both hands, get a firm grip on the entrails and pull down hard removing everything from the body cavity.

At this point the heart and liver should be salvaged and put in plastic bags brought along for this purpose. If water is immediately available they should be rinsed and as much excess blood removed as possible before sealing them in the bags.

Quickly lift the carcass by its hind legs and place a rock or log under its rump causing the back legs to spread open. With your knife blade locate the seam in the pelvis and cut through the bone. You may have to hit the knife blade with a rock. This will cause the hind legs to lay even farther apart, making cleaning easier. Wipe the cavity dry, and pay particular attention to the cleaning of the wound area. Now the tongue may be salvaged. It should be washed, scraped, and hanged to drain and cool.

If a tree and rope are available the animal should be hanged by its head or antlers for about 20 minutes to allow any loose blood to drain out of the body cavity. If no tree is available then turn the carcass upside down on a clean place on the ground.

If the animal must be carried a long distance back to camp, the skin is best left on to protect it in the dragging or carrying process, or from rain or snow. However, if the weather is warm the skin should be removed as soon as possible, and the carcass hanged in an airy place and covered with some kind of light cloth to protect it from dust and flies until you can return for it. Since the skin is most easily removed while the carcass is still warm, the animal should be skinned within two hours after it is killed. Cut the skin down the inside of each leg to the middle of the animal. Cut around the neck as close to the head as possible. Grasping the skin with both hands at the back of the head, pull down hard removing the skin down to the front legs. Use your knife to work the skin off around the legs and continue to pull the skin down the back until it is completely removed at the tail.

After skinning, hang the carcass by its hind legs and prop the body cavity open with a stick to let it cool. If it is hanged by its antlers, the blood still in the smaller veins will collect in the hams and cause a greater opportunity for meat spoilage. Cover the carcass with a light cloth and allow to hang for five to six hours.

DO NOT transport the unskinned animal long distances on the fender or hood of your car. Motor heat and exposure of the unprocessed meat can only hasten spoilage, or at the very least, give the meat a stale taste.

Small Game

Since all game is easier to skin and dress when it is warm, small game also should be dressed in the field. Remove the scent glands from rabbits, opossums, and raccoons. Slit from the breast bone to the tail. Hold front legs in one hand and hindquarters in the other and shake out entrails. Remove head and tail, and cut all legs off at the first joint. Cut the pelt around the rear leg at the hock. Cut on the inside of the leg to the tail and pull the pelt down over the carcass. Most peel rather easily. Wipe cavity with clean cloth, and place in salt water as soon as possible.

It should be noted that rabbits, squirrels, and opossums are all subject to the disease tularemia which causes a high fever of several weeks in humans. You may be infected by a germ entering your blood stream through a cut or scratch. To guard against this, always wash thoroughly after dressing these animals. Of course any animal having tularemia (which is recognizable by a spotted liver) is not edible and must be discarded.

Game Birds

Both game birds and waterfowl should be dressed as soon as possible, unless you are planning to hang them to ripen. Birds should always be picked dry, never scalded, and feathers pulled downward, the way they grow. Pinfeathers may be removed after you have gotten the birds home by singeing them over a slow flame. Another method of removing feathers and down is with hot paraffin. Dip the bird in hot paraffin, then in cold water. Peel paraffin off with feathers in chunks. Strain paraffin to re-use.

After plucking, remove the oil sac above the tail. Remove the head half way up the neck. Slit the skin on the neck big enough to pull out the windpipe, gullet, and voice box. Slit down from end of breast bone to tail. Remove the entrails. Do not break the gall bladder which is fastened to the liver or the bile will ruin the meat. Save the liver, heart, and gizzard. Peel or cut the lining from the gizzard. Cut off wings at first joint, and then wipe out the body cavity with clean cloth. After you have the birds home and are giving them a more thorough cleaning, be sure to check closely for any shot which may have remained lodged in the flesh.

Processing Wild Game

Because of increasingly strict state laws more and more locker plants are refusing to process wild game, much of which has been improperly field dressed long in advance of their receiving it. Though many locker plants will still process your meat, hunting season is the busiest time of the year for these people, and you may not always find available facilities when you need them.

An alternative to this dilemma is processing the meat yourself. It is not a difficult job if you have the right tools and equipment and have planned ahead of your hunting trip. Good sharp knives are imperative: a 6-inch curved skinning knife, a narrow-bladed boning knife, a cleaver, and a meat saw are adequate tools.

Cleanliness is always important. You should choose an indoor location to do the actual butchering and have a strong table handy with plenty of working space on it. The carcass must be suspended from sturdy hooks by its hind legs. Be sure it is well secured because you will be putting the carcass under a great deal of pressure. The neck should be removed first by severing it at a right angle to the backbone just in front of the shoulder blade. Using your meat cleaver, split the pelvic bone and the breast bone down the center. Next divide the carcass in halves by sawing through the middle of the spinal column.

Take down one half from its hook and place it on your table to cut it into smaller sections. The forequarter should be removed by cutting the carcass through just behind the shoulder blade; the hindquarter is removed by cutting just in front of the pelvic bone. The remaining part is the midsection. These sections should be wiped clean with a damp cloth to remove any hair or bone chips.

From the forequarter the leg should be cut off just below the shoulder joint and again at the remaining joint. The upper part may be boned and cut into roasts while the lower part, or shank, may be used for hamburger or stew meat. (For information about which meat cuts provide the best stew meat, see the introduction to the stew recipes section.)

From the hindquarter the leg, or haunch, should be severed from the rump by cutting just below the joint where they join. The rump may be cut into roasts or steaks, and the leg may provide round steaks, leg roasts, or tender stew meat. Again, the shank may be used for stew meat.

From the midsection you may have either rib roasts or chops. The flank, or stomach, meat should be cut away first and reserved for stew meat or hamburger. For spare ribs cut across the lower portion of the ribs. For chops slice between the ribs and then sever the backbone with the meat cleaver. The same should be done with the loin chops though, of course, there will be no ribs. Only the neck is left which may be boned completely and cut into small pieces for stew or hamburger meat.

Be sure to remove all excess fat from butchered meat as it is the main contributor to the wild or gamey flavor which often permeates the meat. The kind of wrapping paper you use and the way you use it is very important. Heavy, plastic-coated paper is a must to prevent air seepage which, if allowed, will result in freezer burn. Double wrapping makes a bulkier but safer package and should always be secured with freezer tape. Each package should be weighed, and its contents and the date marked clearly with grease pencil or ink marker. After the meat is packaged it should be frozen immediately at 0° or below.

Hints on Freezing and Storing Wild Game

Meat carcasses should be chilled quickly to 40° or lower within 24 hours after they have been field dressed. Then hang and chill meat at 35° (this temperature is maintained at locker plants). Most large game animals should be hanged, or cured, at this temperature for at least two weeks before processing.

Small birds and ducks may be placed in wax-coated milk cartons, covered with water and frozen. If birds are not to be frozen they should be dressed, drawn, and then chilled for 12 hours before cooking.

The following are recommended time limits for usage of meat stored at 0°:

Roasts and steaks	**8-12 months**
Chops (antelope, javelina, etc.)	**4-6 months**
Ground Meat	**3-4 months**
Stew Meat	**6-8 months**
Sausage, lunch meats	**2-3 months**
Game birds, rabbits	**6-8 months**
Giblets (birds)	**3-4 months**
Heart, liver, tongue	**4-6 months**

Allow frozen meat to thaw in the refrigerator, and use within 24 hours.

Cooked meats and casseroles may be refrozen if allowed to cool and are packed tightly.

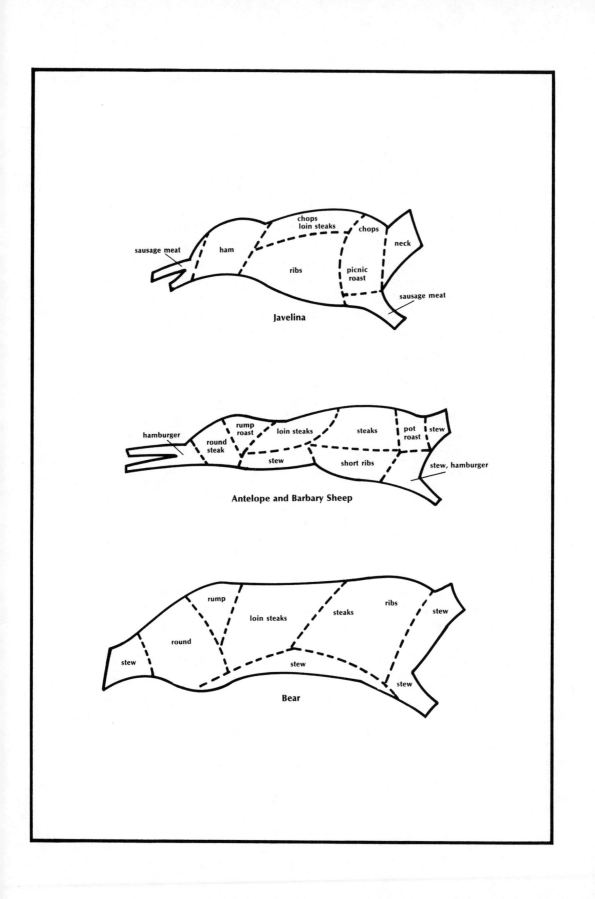

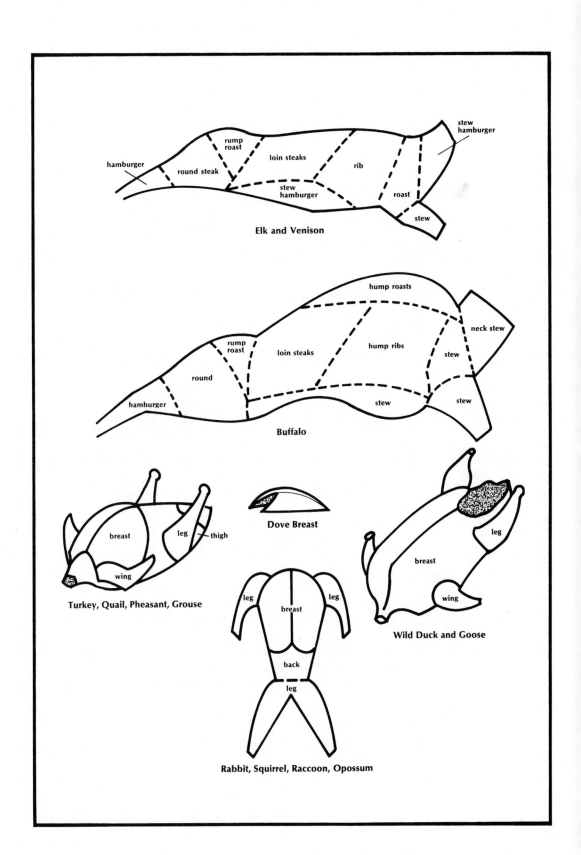

Elk and Venison

hamburger · round steak · rump roast · loin steaks · stew hamburger · rib · roast · stew · stew hamburger

Buffalo

hamburger · round · rump roast · loin steaks · hump roasts · hump ribs · neck stew · stew · stew · stew

breast · leg · thigh · wing

Turkey, Quail, Pheasant, Grouse

Dove Breast

leg · breast · wing

Wild Duck and Goose

leg · breast · leg · back · leg

Rabbit, Squirrel, Raccoon, Opossum

Canning

If you find that your freezer will not hold all the game you had planned to freeze, you might try canning a portion of your meat. All you need is a large size pressure cooker. Nearly every kind of wild game, including birds, can be canned in either of the two methods available:

Cold pack: Soak meat in salt water (⅓ cup salt to 1 quart water) for 2 or more hours. Drain. Remove all bone (except in the case of game birds) gristle, and all fat. Cut meat into pieces small enough to go in jars. Pack loosely in sterilized jars, leaving 1 inch space at top. Set open jars in deep pan. Add water to within 1 inch of top of jar. Cover pan. Simmer until medium done (about 1½ hours). Add 1 tablespoon salt to each jar, add water if needed to cover meat. Screw on lids and process according to the directions which come with your particular pressure cooker.

Hot pack: Soak meat in salt water as for cold pack. Drain, cut into pieces. Cook meat in covered kettle until medium done (about 1½ hours). Pack loosely in sterilized jars. Add 1 tablespoon salt. Cover with enough broth or boiling water to cover meat. Screw on lids and process according to the directions which come with your particular pressure cooker.

Most pressure cookers require: 75 minutes at 10 lb. pressure for pints. 90 minutes at 10 lb. pressure for quarts.

Corning

See recipe for corned elk. Large pieces of almost any other game may be corned by this method.

Drying

Jerky: Jerky has become quite popular as a novelty food for snacks and entertaining. It is highly nourishing, easy to prepare, and contains very few calories.

1) Cut fresh (never frozen) venison or other game (tender cuts with no fat) into ⅛ inch thin strips. Cut across the grain for tender jerky.

2) Sprinkle generously (do not rub in) with salt. Add freshly ground (fine) pepper to taste (you may use other spices
in addition to the salt and pepper, such as garlic powder,
savory, marjoram, curry, basil, etc.).

3) Place on rack of broiler pan so meat juices can drip away
from meat as it dries.

4) Place in low oven (120°). Prop oven door open 2 inches
to allow moisture to escape.

5) Dry for 8 hours or to desired doneness.

6) To store put in cool dry place. Do not store in a closed
container because it may mold.

Jerky may also be sun-dried by hanging strips of meat over
a clothesline and covering with cheesecloth. Leave 8 hours
or more depending on the extent of sunlight.

Pemmican: Pemmican is an old Indian recipe in-
tended to contain the most possible nourishment in the
smallest possible package. It is an excellent emergency
ration, and can be carried easily by hikers, boaters, and
campers.

1) Cut pieces of lean, tender game meat across the grain.

2) Soak in hot brine for ½ to 1 hour. Proportion: ½ cup
salt to 1 gallon water.

3) Drain and place on broiler rack in low oven (120°) for
8-12 hours or until very dry. Prop oven door open 2 inches
to allow moisture to escape.

4) Remove and pound or grind into powder.

5) Add hot fat (any that does not require refrigeration) to
make a thick dough. Season with salt, freshly ground pepper, and any other seasoning you wish such as cinnamon.

6) Grind, or cut finely, any dried fruit (apricots, apples,
etc.) and add to dough.

7) Make into small loaves. Tie in cheesecloth, and dip in
hot paraffin to waterproof.

Seasonings

SEASONINGS

monosodium glutamate: a chemical which intensifies the natural flavor of most food. Originally extracted from seaweed, the major sources are now sugar beets, corn, and wheat. It is often marketed under its abbreviation MSG.

peppercorns: the whole dried berry of the pepper plant. They are used for cooking while the ground variety is used for seasoning.

saltpeter: known as rock salt because it exudes from rocks. It is also called **chile saltpeter.**

Spices

Spices come from seeds, stems, roots and barks, leaves, buds and fruit. Most of these grow in the tropic. They are always dried and are available whole, coarsely ground, or pulverized. Some spices are sweet, some hot, some pungent.

allspice: the dried, unripe fruit of a pepper tree. It resembles the flavor of a blend of clove, cinnamon, and nutmeg.

Angostura bitters: comes from the bark of a tree in the rue family. It is aromatic and is sometimes used in the preparation of liqueurs.

caraway seed: the dried fruit of a plant of the carrot family. It has a tangy flavor.

cayenne: the ground, dried pod of dried capsicum.

chili pepper: the dried pod of dried capsicum which is very hot.

cinnamon: the inner bark of the cassia tree, very aromatic.

cloves: or **spice nails:** the dried buds of the clove tree. Their pungent, almost hot flavor intensifies on standing.

cumin seeds: the dried fruit of a shrub. It has a strong flavor and is a basic ingredient in both chili powder and curry powder.

curry powder: a blend of many spices and herbs. Different brands vary in strength. Use sparingly for best results.

fennel seeds: the aromatic, dried fruit or seed of a plant of the parsley family. They have a slight licorice flavor.

horseradish: a grated root used as a condiment and frequently combined with vinegar.

ginger: one of the few spices which grows below the ground. Rich and extremely pungent in flavor, its taste is hot and clean.

juniper berries: the fruit of the juniper tree, which is an evergreen. They are considered indispensable for game cookery.

mace: the dried outer covering of the fruit of the nutmeg tree. It is similar to nutmeg in flavor but more delicate.

mustard: ground and mixed with herbs and vinegar to make commercially prepared mustard, sometimes called wet mustard. Dry mustard has a sharp, pungent flavor and is used as a condiment and flavoring aid. "Dijon" mustard has a different flavor than prepared or dried mustard. It is creamier and may be hot or mild.

nutmeg: the dried seed of a tropical tree. It is sweet in flavor and highly spicy.

paprika: the sweetest of the ground red peppers. It is slightly aromatic and an excellent source of vitamin C.

piñon nuts: the seeds from various pine trees.

saffron: a costly spice taken from the stigmas of a particular kind of crocus. It is a bright golden color with an exotic taste and is potent so should be used sparingly.

sesame seeds: give a rich nutlike flavor and may be used as nuts would be.

Herbs

Herbs are soft, succulent plants, often growing in a temperate climate. They are invaluable for flavoring and seasoning food, and fall in two general categories; STRONG: marjoram, basil, mint, sage, rosemary, thyme, tarragon, dill, oregano, and bay; MILD: savory, chervil, chives, and parsley. Many herbs may be grown easily almost anywhere and take little space in a garden. Herbs may be used either fresh or dried, the dried ones being available as leaves, whole or crushed, or ground powder. When using fresh herbs, two to four times as much as dried is necessary, 1 tablespoon of fresh equaling about 1 teaspoon of dried.

Do not hesitate to experiment with herbs. You may find that variations in many of these recipes achieve a flavor more to your own tastes.

basil: a member of the mint family with an aromatic, clovelike scent. It is pungent.

bay leaves: the dried leaves of the laurel or sweet bay tree. Their flavor is strong and pungent so use sparingly.

celery seeds: are not related to the vegetable celery. They are a wild variety of celery know as smallage.

chervil: resembles a delicate parsley, with a flavor similar to tarragon.

chives: the tiniest member of the onion family. They are usually used fresh and may be used instead of onions for flavoring.

garlic: a bulb of the lily family. The juice of fresh garlic contains most of the flavor. **Garlic powder** or **garlic salt** can be used instead of the fresh.

marjoram: a member of the mint family. It has a flavor more delicate than oregano.

oregano: also known as wild marjoram. It is more pungent than marjoram and is used more often.

parsley: the best known and best loved herb. The flat leaf type has a more pungent flavor, while the curly leaf is more decorative. Fresh parsley will keep 10 days in a refrigerator if tightly covered.

rosemary: a member of the mint family. The dried leaves look like miniature pine needles and are pungent.

sage: should be used with discretion because its flavor is bitter, astringent, and at the same time fragrant.

savory: more delicate than sage and combines well with other herbs. There are both "winter" and "summer" savory. The winter variety is stronger in flavor.

tarragon: has a strong flavor of anise or licorice. Since its flavor dominates most others, it is best used alone.

thyme: a member of the mint family and has a warm, aromatic, and slightly pungent flavor.

WINES

Wine should never overpower the taste of the food. It adds zest to veal or fish, and when used to marinate meats, wine tenderizes and brings out the flavor. In cooking, the alcohol evaporates with the heat and only the flavor remains.

Red table or dinner wine is used for red meats and game; the lighter-bodied red wine for ham, pork, roast duckling, or lamb dishes. A white table or dinner wine is used for meats such as veal, turkey, or chicken. Sherry and Madeira are excellent to flavor soups and sauces.

As with spices and seasonings every individual should use wine to his own particular taste. None of the wines in these recipes are arbitrarily given and in each case a similar wine may be used to suit the cook's personal preferences in flavor.

Table of Equivalent Weights and Measures

3 teaspoons = 1 tablespoon
4 tablespoons = ¼ cup
5⅓ tablespoons = ⅓ cup
8 tablespoons = ½ cup
10⅔ tablespoons = ⅔ cup
12 tablespoons = ¾ cup
16 tablespoons = 1 cup
2 tablespoons = 1 ounce
8 ounces = 1 cup
32 ounces = 1 quart
16 ounces = 1 pound
2 cups = 1 pound
2 cups = 1 pint
2 pints = 1 quart
4 quarts = 1 gallon
8 quarts = 1 peck
4 pecks = 1 bushel

Game Birds

**Dove
Quail
Duck
Goose
Turkey
Pheasant
Grouse**

Dove

Dove should be dressed by merely skinning out the breast and discarding the rest, for there is little meat on the rest of the bird. Dove meat has a bland flavor, more like pheasant, and is always tender and moist. It should be cooked in a sauce. The breast meat is darker than chicken but has no gamey taste. Because dove season is held in the warmer months, the birds should be dressed and chilled immediately.

Braised Breast of Dove with Mushrooms

8 breasts	¼ cup cooking oil
⅓ cup flour	½ cup Marsala wine
½ teaspoon salt	1 can (2 oz.) button
¼ teaspoon pepper	mushrooms

Dredge dove breasts in seasoned flour. Turn to brown on all sides in heavy skillet in hot cooking oil. Reduce heat. Simmer 30 minutes or until tender. Add mushrooms and wine, and heat throughly. Do not boil. Serve with hot buttered rice. Serves 4.

Breast of Dove Casserole

8 breasts	1 package (8 oz.) noodles
¼ cup cooking oil	3 cups boiling water
1 can (10½ oz.) cream	1 teaspoon salt
of mushroom soup	3 tablespoons butter
¼ cup grated Parmesan	¼ cup chopped parsley
cheese	

Cook noodles in boiling, salted water until tender according to directions on package. Drain. Stir in butter and parsley. Place in casserole. Set aside.

Brown dove breasts on all sides in the hot cooking oil. Drain. Place dove breasts on noodles in casserole. Cover with mushroom soup. Sprinkle with Parmesan cheese. Cover casserole. Bake in 350° oven 40 minutes. Serves 4.

Creamed Dove on Toast Points

Use 5-6 breasts. Place in pressure cooker and cover with water. Add 1 teaspoon salt, 2 stalks sliced celery, pinch of rosemary. Cook at medium pressure 15-20 minutes. Cool. Remove from liquid. Cut into cubes.

Melt 3 tablespoons shortening or butter. Stir in 3 tablespoons flour, 1 teaspoon salt and ¼ teaspoon pepper. Remove from heat and stir in 1 can (14 oz.) chicken broth and 1 cup cream or top milk. Heat slowly and stir until thickened. Stir in the cubed dove meat and 2 tablespoons sherry wine. Serve over toast points. Serves 6.

Dove Roll-Ups

8 deboned breasts	1 cup chicken broth
1 package Spanish rice and vermicelli mix	¼ cup dry white wine
1 can (16 oz.) tomatoes	1 can (2 oz.) chopped mushrooms
½ teaspoon salt	1 cup diced ham
¼ teaspoon pepper	2 tablespoons chopped parsley
¼ cup butter	

Flatten deboned breasts. Prepare Spanish rice mix using the can of tomatoes instead of liquid. Heap spoonfuls of rice mixture on each of the breasts. Roll up and fasten with toothpick or small skewers. Sprinkle with salt and pepper. Brown slowly on both sides in butter. Add broth. Cover and cook over low heat 40 minutes or until tender. Place on hot platter and remove picks.

Add wine, mushrooms, ham, and parsley to drippings in pan. Heat and spoon sauce over breasts. Serves 4.

Quail

Quail have light, dry meat, very fine textured, and

not at all gamey. Although the quail is small the whole bird is cooked. The quail should be plucked or skinned and dressed as soon as they are shot, not when you have accumulated your limit. Leave in the air or cool as soon as possible. Remove oil sac and soak in salt water 3-4 hours.

Broiled quail is delicious. An excellent marinade for quail is made witth ½ cup soy sauce, ½ cup white wine, ¼ cup brown sugar, and 1 teaspoon ginger. This is enough marinade for 4 quail and will serve 4 people. Let the quail stand in the marinade 4 hours. Salt and broil over hot coals, basting often with marinade.

Grilled Quail

Cut quail down the back. Flatten with hammer or cleaver. Marinate in a mixture of 1 cup Burgundy wine, 1 minced garlic clove, and 1 sliced onion 3-4 hours or overnight in the refrigerator. Remove from marinade and dry. Roll in fine bread crumbs and brown under broiler 30 minutes turning several times. Strain marinade. Simmer down to ½ cup. Mix with ½ cup melted butter and pour over the quail.

Broiled Quail

Split quail in halves. Sprinkle with salt and pepper. Broil over hot coals basting frequently with a mixture of melted butter and 1 tablespoon lemon juice. Cook 15-20 minutes per side or to desired doneness. Serve over wild rice.

Quail with White Grapes

Rub the inside of 6 quail with salt and pepper. Put 6-8 peeled, white grapes inside each quail. Place each quail on a square of heavy-duty aluminum foil. Pour melted butter over each quail. Wrap loosely and place in an uncovered roasting pan. Roast in 350° oven 30-40 minutes. Uncover during the last 15 minutes to brown. Remove to hot platter. Pour juices from the alumium tents into pan.

Skim off fat. Add ¼ cup white wine, 1 chicken bouillon cube, and 1 cup water. Simmer gently. Add about 30 peeled, white grapes. Season and serve sauce over birds. Serves 4.

Quail Gabriel

Cut 6 quail in half. Brown on both sides in 2 tablespoons salad oil. Remove quail. Add to juices in pan 3 cans (8 oz. each) tomato sauce and 3 cans water. Add 1 can (6 oz.) tomato paste, 1 teaspoon salt, ½ teaspoon pepper, ½ teaspoon oregano, 1 minced garlic clove, and 1 tablespoon parsley. Cook over low heat 15 minutes. Return quail to pan. Add 1 can (4 oz.) mushrooms. Cover and simmer 1½-2 hours or until very tender. Add more water if needed. Serve over hot, boiled, buttered spaghetti. Serves 4-6.

Potted Quail

Rub inside and out of 6 quail with salt and pepper. Sauté 1 sliced onion in 1 tablespoon butter. Combine with 1 can (4 oz.) sliced mushrooms. Fill cavity of birds with this mixture. Mix 1 can (10½ oz.) cream of chicken soup with ½ cup Marsala wine. Pour sauce over quail in deep casserole. Cover and bake in 350° oven 1 hour. Baste occasionally with the sauce. Serves 4.

Quail Hawaiian

6-8 quail	1 tablespoon cornstarch
2 tablespoons cooking oil	¼ teaspoon curry
1 teaspoon salt	powder
1 cup pineapple juice	1 tablespoon sugar
2 tablespoons lemon	Slivered almonds
juice	

Split quail in half. Sprinkle with salt. Brown on both sides in hot fat in heavy skillet. Remove quail from pan. Combine juices, cornstarch, curry, and sugar and stir into the juices in pan. Cook over low heat, stirring constantly, until thickened. Return quail to pan. Spoon sauce over quail and simmer 30 minutes. Serve on toast or rice. Top with slivered almonds. Serves 4.

Quail Casserole

Marinate 6-8 quail in a mixture of 1 cup port wine, 1 teaspoon salt, ¼ teaspoon pepper, ½ teaspoon nutmeg, and 1 crumbled bay leaf 4-6 hours or overnight. Remove birds. Strain marinade.

Line the bottom of a deep, greased casserole with thinly sliced ham. Sprinkle over ham 1 tablespoon chopped onion, 2 tablespoons chopped parsley, and 1 can (2 oz.) mushrooms. Place quail on this mixture. Add 6 carrots cut into sticks and 12 small, whole onions. Mix marinade with 1 can (10½ oz.) chicken gravy and pour over all. Cover casserole and bake in 350° oven 40-50 minutes or until tender. Serves 4.

Duck

Because the first few weeks of duck hunting season are during warm weather, every precaution must be taken so the birds will be in good condition when you get them home. Always remove the entrails and cool the ducks as soon as possible. Stuff the cavity with wet grass. Do not put undrawn birds in a hunting coat or bag and leave them all day. Clotted blood from the shot or partly digested food will ruin the flesh and spoil the flavor.

Freshly killed ducks tend to be tough, so it is a good idea to hang the birds for 2-4 days in a cool dry place. If they are to be hanged, they should not be plucked until ripening period is over. Never cook any bird without removing the oil sac, a triangular piece of skin at the base of the tail containing the oil glands. Remove any pinfeathers with tweezers. They are easier to remove after the bird has been frozen. Singe off fuzz. Wash giblets in soda water and rinse.

To remove some of the wild flavor from ducks, soak in soda or onion water for 1 hour and place peeled, quartered apples in the cavity. Discard apples after cooking. Some people prefer ducks rare, without stuffing. If this is the case, roast a large duck only about an hour in the oven (425°) and baste with red wine.

Charcoaled Teal

Teal are delicious when split, seasoned, and basted with butter over hot charcoal on a barbecue grill. Make sure the rack is over 3 inches from the coals. They may also be left whole and threaded on a spit. Baste often with melted butter. Should be done in 30 minutes.

Duck with Orange

This recipe requires 1 large or 2 small ducks per person.

4 large or 8 small ducks	orange rind
2 peeled, quartered apples	2 tablespoons orange juice
1 teaspoon salt	2 cans (10½ oz. each) cream of chicken soup
¼ teaspoon pepper	
1 minced garlic clove	
½ teaspoon grated	

Cover ducks, apples, and garlic with water and simmer 3 hours. For small ducks 2 hours should be sufficient. The meat should fall from the bones. If you are in a hurry, use a pressure cooker for 30 minutes.

Remove ducks from broth and allow to cool. Remove apples and discard. Cook broth down to 1 cup and strain off fat.

Remove skin and bones and any shot from ducks. Cut into large slices. Place in chafing dish or electric buffet pan. Season with salt and pepper. Mix chicken soup, reserved broth, orange rind, and orange juice. Pour mixture over duck and simmer in serving pan until thickened. Serves 6-8.

Breast of Duck on Wild Rice

Debone ducks by cutting along breast bone ridge. Simmer the remainder and use in other recipes, such as Salmi of Duck or Scalloped Duck.

4-6 breasts
1-2 quartered, unpeeled
  apples
1 teaspoon salt
¼ teaspoon pepper

1 cup melted butter
1 package wild rice
1 can (4 oz.) mushroom
  caps

Place one whole duck breast on a square of heavy-duty aluminum foil. Place 1 quarter apple on top of duck. Season with salt and pepper. Pour melted butter over duck. Bring foil up and seal using one tent per breast. Bake in 350° preheated oven 30-40 minutes. Prepare wild rice as directed on package. Place duck breasts on platter. Surround with wild rice and heated mushroom caps. Serves 4-6.

Roast Duck

Make sure ducks are cleaned, free of pin feathers, and free of shot. Adjust cooking time proportionally to the size of the duck.

3 large or 4 small ducks
3-4 quartered, unpeeled
  apples
6-8 slices bacon
½ cup Burgundy wine

Orange slices or cran-
  berry filled orange cups

Place 1 quartered apple in each duck cavity. Wrap each duck with 2 slices bacon. Place in uncovered roasting pan or dutch oven. Cover with wine and roast in 350° oven 1½-2 hours for well done, 30-40 minutes for rare to medium. Discard apples, place on hot platter, and garnish with orange slices or orange cups. Serves 8.

Stuffed Roast Duck

Prepare ducks as in Roast Duck recipe, omitting

the apple and using any stuffing recipe. If cooking ducks rare, precook the stuffing.

Broiled Duck with Ham

This is an excellent recipe for using small ducks. The combination of flavors is distinctive.

4-6 ducks	½ cup melted butter
1 teaspoon salt	8-12 slices boneless ham
½ teaspoon fresh,	2 cans (10¾ oz. each)
ground peppercorns	beef gravy
Pinch of marjoram	¼ cup white wine

Split ducks in half. Mix melted butter with salt, pepper, and marjoram. Baste ducks with this mixture. Place on grill over hot coals. Turn and baste frequently. Just before done, place ham slices on grill turning to heat. Meanwhile heat beef gravy. Add wine and simmer. Place 1 duck half on piece of ham. Cover with sauce. Serve with rice. Serves 8-10.

Apricot Duck

2-3 ducks	1 can (29 oz.) whole
1 teaspoon salt	apricots
¼ teaspoon pepper	¼ cup white wine
½ cup melted butter	¼ cup water

Wipe ducks dry. Sprinkle inside and out with salt and pepper. Place each duck on heavy-duty foil. Cover birds with melted butter. Pour half of the apricot juice over ducks. Bring foil up and seal. Roast in 350° oven 1½ hours. Uncover, add remaining apricot juice and roast ½ hour more or until nicely browned. Remove ducks and pour juices into pan. Strain off fat. Add wine and water and season to taste. Simmer 5 minutes. Strain into sauceboat. Arrange whole apricots around duck on hot platter. Serves 4-6.

Duck A La Craig

3-4 ducks	1 quartered apple

½ teaspoon salt	3 tablespoons orange
¼ teaspoon pepper	juice
½ teaspoon garlic salt	½ cup Burgundy wine
½ teaspoon grated	1½ tablespoons flour
orange rind	2 tablespoons butter

Place ducks in a pressure cooker. Cover with water and add salt, pepper, and garlic salt. Place apples on top. Pressure cook 30-40 minutes. Remove ducks and apples from broth and cool. Remove skin and bones. Slice duck. Remove fat from broth. Make a roux of flour and butter. Add to broth and stir until smooth. Add orange rind, orange juice, and wine. Simmer slowly until thickened. Add duck slices and heat. Serve on hot platter garnished with orange slices. Serves 6.

Salmi of Duck

2 cups diced, cold,	2 finely chopped green
boiled, or roast duck	onions
1 can (10¾ oz.) duck	Pinch thyme
gravy or beef gravy	Pinch rosemary
½ cup sherry	2 tablespoons butter
1 can (3½ oz.) sliced,	1 teaspoon salt
pitted, ripe olives	¼ teaspoon pepper
1 tablespoon lemon juice	

Sauté onions in butter until transparent. Add duck, olives, gravy, and seasonings. Simmer 5-10 minutes. Add lemon juice and sherry. Simmer 5 minutes more and serve on rice or toast points. Serves 4-6.

Duck Creole

Simmer 2-3 ducks until tender, 3-4 hours. Remove skin and bone and cut into cubes, or use cubed left-over duck.

2 cups or more cubed	2 tablespoons minced
duck	onion
2 tablespoons butter	1 cup chopped ham
1½ tablespoons flour	1 teaspoon salt

½ teaspoon pepper
1 teaspoon paprika
2 tablespoons chopped,
    sweet, green pepper
½ cup chopped celery
½ tablespoon chopped

parsley
1 can (10½ oz.) chicken
    consommé
1 whole clove
¼ teaspoon mace
1 can (8 oz.) tomato sauce

Melt butter, add flour. Stir until smooth. Add consomme, salt, pepper, paprika, onion, green pepper, celery, parsley, clove, and mace. Simmer 30 minutes, stirring occasionally, and adding water if needed. Stir in ham and duck. Add tomato sauce. Heat thoroughly and serve over hot buttered rice. Serves 6.

Scalloped Duck

3-4 cups cold, diced duck
6 slices bacon
2 tablespoons butter
2 tablespoons chopped
    onion
3 tablespoons chopped
    green pepper
¼ cup flour
2 cups broth or chicken

consommé
1 cup light cream
1 can (4 oz.) mushrooms
1 teaspoon salt
¼ teaspoon pepper
⅓ cup Marsala wine
2 tablespoons chopped
    parsley

Cook bacon until crisp. Break into small pieces. Add butter, onion, and green pepper to bacon fat. Cook until soft, but not brown. Blend in flour. Combine broth, cream, and liquid from mushrooms. Stir in and cook until thickened. Add duck, mushrooms, salt, pepper, and wine. Heat, but do not boil. Put in serving dish and sprinkle with bacon bits and parsley. Serves 6-8.

Goose

Follow the cleaning and hanging method for ducks. Wild geese have all dark, lean meat with less fat than domestic geese. The young geese are delicious and less wild tasting than duck. If the bird is old, parboil or cut into serving pieces and pressure until tender.

Roast Goose in Paper Bag

Stuff goose with bread, cornbread, or any favorite dressing. Tie goose (do not use skewers). Do not salt. Rub entire bird with cooking oil, butter, or shortening. Place in heavy, brown, paper bag. Fold end over and staple shut making it air tight. Roast in uncovered baking pan at 300° 5-6 hours depending on size of the bird. Boil the neck and giblets. Chop and add to canned chicken or turkey gravy.

Roast Goose with Fruit Stuffing

Soak 15 prunes in sherry wine 6 hours. Simmer them in the wine until soft. Pit and chop. Peel, core, and chop 6 apples. Mix the apples with the prunes, wine, and add 1 teaspoon salt.

Wipe off the goose. Stuff the bird with the fruit stuffing. Tie the bird. Place on heavy-duty foil. Cover with melted butter. Bring the foil up and seal. Place in pan and roast in 350° oven 35 minutes per pound. (Wild goose should be cooked longer than tame). Meanwhile cook neck and giblets in salted water until tender. Chop and sauté with 1 small chopped onion in butter. Reserve liquid.

When goose is done, remove foil and place on hot platter. Strain fat from pan juices. Make a roux of 4 tablespoons butter and 2 tablespoons flour. Stir into the reserved liquid and pan juices. Stir in the chopped giblets. Cook slowly stirring constantly. Add more water if necessary and season to taste.

Goose Liver Pâté

Simmer goose liver in salted water. Add 3 slices onion and 1 garlic clove. Cook slowly 1 hour. Remove liver and discard onion and garlic. Mash liver and mix with 1 finely diced, hard-boiled egg and enough mayonnaise to moisten.

Gourmet Goose

This is a very good way to use up the leftover roast goose.

2-3 cups diced, cooked goose	**1 minced garlic clove**
2 tablespoons butter	**1 can (10½ oz.) cream of chicken soup**
½ cup chopped green onions	**½ cup sherry**
½ cup chopped celery	**2 cups cooked noodles**
	½ cup Parmesan cheese

Sauté onions, celery, and garlic in butter. Mix with soup and sherry. Alternate layers of goose, noodles, and soup mixture in greased casserole. Top with Parmesan cheese. Bake for 40 minutes in 275° oven. Serves 4-6.

Turkey

Wild turkeys are very different from the domestic variety, having all dark meat which is much more moist. They have deeper breasts and longer legs. The meat is fine grained and has no wild taste. The bird should be plucked as soon as killed, and dressed as soon as possible. Always test for doneness with a meat thermometer (180°) because the meat will not feel soft, and you cannot move the leg easily as with domestic turkey. Young gobblers and hens are very tender and delicious when roasted or broiled.

Broiled Turkey

Use a small bird, weighing not more than 5 pounds. Cut into 4 pieces. Flatten with a cleaver. Preheat broiler. Place pieces of turkey on the rack skin side down. Sprinkle with salt and pepper and baste occasionally with a mixture of melted butter, lemon juice, and 1 minced garlic clove. Broil slowly turning with tongs occasionally. Cook 1 hour. Test for doneness.

The turkey may also be broiled over charcoal, using the butter sauce or a barbecue sauce. Allow the same cooking time. Serves 4-6.

Roast Wild Turkey

Use a young hen or gobbler. After picking and dressing, soak in salt water for several hours. Rub cavity with salt and pepper. Stuff if desired. Truss the bird as for regular turkey. Place on heavy-duty foil. Pour ½ cup melted butter over the bird. Bring foil up and seal. Roast in 400° preheated oven 4-6 hours depending on weight of the bird, allow 30-35 minutes per pound. Test with meat thermometer, and cook to 180°. Uncover and roast until bird browns evenly. Pour off drippings from alumimum tent. Skim off fat. Add 1 can chicken or giblet gravy. Stir until thickened.

Wild Turkey with Chestnut Stuffings

1 turkey 8-10 pounds	2 tablespoons chopped
2 tablespoons butter	parsley
1 cup chopped onion	½ teaspoon salt
1 cup diced celery	¼ teaspoon pepper
½ pound sausage	½ cup butter
2 cups bread crumbs	
2 cups cooked, peeled, and chopped chestnuts	

Melt 2 tablespoons butter in skillet. Sauté onion and celery until limp. Add sausage meat. Cook over low heat stirring and separating meat until done. Drain off all fat. Lightly mix in bread crumbs, chestnuts, parsley, salt, and pepper. Spoon stuffing into neck and body cavities. Sew up openings. Truss. Place in roasting pan. Brush with melted butter. Place in 400° preheated oven. Roast 30 minutes. Reduce heat to 350° and roast for 2½ more hours or until meat thermometer reads 180°. Baste frequently with butter. Remove turkey to hot platter. Skim off fat. Thicken drippings with corn starch. Add cold water. Cook, stirring constantly until thickened. Serves 10-12.

Poached Turkey (Recommended for an older bird)

In the bottom of a roasting pan on a rack, place 3 slices of salt pork. Cover with 2 chopped carrots, 2 sliced onions, 2 chopped stalks of celery, 1 tablespoon parsley, a pinch of thyme, 1 mashed garlic clove, and 1 bay leaf.

Rub turkey inside and out with salt and pepper. Truss the bird. Place on vegetables. Pour ½ cup melted butter over turkey. Pour 1 can chicken broth and 2 cups white wine into pan. Cover roasting pan and simmer over low heat on top of stove adding water as needed. Steam 6-8 hours or until very tender. Remove turkey to hot platter. Remove turkey to hot platter. Remove and discard bay leaf and salt pork. Strain off fat. Thicken with a flour paste. Simmer, stirring constantly, until smooth. Adjust seasonings. Serve gravy in gravy boat on side.

Scalloped Turkey

A good way to use up leftovers

2 cups diced, roast turkey	**crumbs**
1 can (10½ oz.) cream of celery soup	**¼ cup crumbled Blue cheese**
1 green pepper sliced thin	**3 tablespoons melted butter**
¼ teaspoon nutmeg	**Salt and pepper**
2 cups toasted bread	

Mix the turkey, celery soup, nutmeg, salt, and pepper. Place 1 cup bread crumbs in a buttered casserole. Add turkey mixture. Sprinkle with cheese. Add the other cup bread crumbs. Cover with melted butter. Bake in 350° oven 35 minutes. Serves 4.

Turkey Supreme

This is an excellent dish and may be made with any leftover game bird or domestic fowl.

2 cups diced, cooked turkey	**1 can (10½ oz.) cream of mushroom soup**

1 cup light cream (or canned milk)
1 teaspoon salt
½ teaspoon freshly ground pepper
1 can (2 oz.) chopped mushrooms
2 cups cooked spaghetti

1 can (4 oz.) chopped pimientos
¼ cup grated Parmesan cheese
¼ cup bread crumbs mixed with
¼ cup melted butter
½ cup white wine

Mix soup, cream, and seasonings. Add turkey, cooked spaghetti, mushrooms, pimientos, and cheese. Stir in white wine. Pour into a buttered casserole or individual ramekins. Top with the buttered bread crumbs. Bake in 300° oven 25 minutes. Increase heat to brown crumbs. Serves 4-6.

Turkey Hash

1½ cups chopped, cooked turkey
1 cup chopped, cooked potatoes
½ cup chopped onion
2 tablespoons butter

1 cup gravy (or 1 can chicken gravy)
½ teaspoon salt
½ teaspoon pepper
¼ cup grated cheese
4-6 eggs

Sauté onion slowly in butter until limp. Add turkey, potatoes, gravy, and seasonings. Cook over low heat until hash is browned turning occasionally. Make hollows in the hash. Slip an egg into each hollow. Cover the pan and cook slowly until eggs are set. Top eggs with shredded cheese. Serves 4.

Turkey Soup

Remove most of the meat from turkey carcass. Break bones and place them in a heavy pan. Cover with water, 1 teaspoon salt, ½ teaspoon freshly ground pepper, 1 garlic clove, and 1 bay leaf. Cover and simmer 1 hour or more. Cool. Remove garlic and bay leaf. Remove skin and bones. Dice remaining meat. Add water to make 2½ quarts. Add 1 cup chopped onion and 1 cup chopped celery. Add 1 chicken bouillon cube. Simmer 30 minutes. Add ½ cup instant rice. Simmer 10 more minutes. Adjust seasonings. Mix 1½ tablespoons flour with enough water to make a smooth paste. Stir in soup and cook until thickened. Serves 8-10.

Pheasant

Care in the field is essential for having a tasty bird. Remove feathers or skin immediately. Dress and chill. If birds are to be hung for ripening they should not be plucked. Soak in salt water for a few hours or overnight. Keep the bird cool. Clean the cavity thoroughly and remove all pinfeathers and singe. Check carefully for shot. Be sure to remove the oil sac as with ducks.

Pheasant meat is light, fine textured, and tends to be a little dry. It has a very delicate flavor without any wild taste at all. A moist cooking method is recommended. Young birds, which are identifiable by their soft, pliable spurs, are very tender while older birds may be tough and should be pressured or braised in a sauce.

Roast Pheasant

Season young pheasant with salt and pepper. Place on heavy-duty aluminum foil. Pour melted butter over the bird. Bring up foil and seal. Roast in 350° oven I hour or until done. Serve with canned chicken gravy. Serves 4.

Braised Marsala Pheasant

1 pheasant	1 can (2 oz.) mushrooms
¼ cup flour	½ cup Marsala wine
½ teaspoon salt	½ cup sliced onion
¼ teaspoon pepper	1 minced garlic clove
Pinch thyme	½ cup cream
3 tablespoons cooking oil	

Cut pheasant into serving pieces. Roll in seasoned flour. Brown in hot oil in heavy pan or dutch oven. Remove pheasant. Brown onion and garlic in pan. Return pheasant to pan. Add mushrooms and wine. Cover pan and roast in 300° oven 1½-2 hours. Remove pheasant to hot platter. Strain off fat. Stir in cream and serve sauce over pheasant. Serve with hot biscuits. Serves 4.

Baron of Pheasant

1-2 pheasants
2-3 tablespoons butter
2-4 thin slices salt pork
1 cup chicken broth (1 bouillon cube dissolved in 1 cup boiling water)
½ teaspoon salt
¼ teaspoon pepper
Pinch each nutmeg,
clove, and thyme
1 bay leaf
½ cup chopped celery
2 tablespoons grated onion
1 tablespoon chopped parsley
2 tablespoons flour
1 can (10½ oz.) chicken broth

Split pheasants. Place the halved birds in heavy pan or dutch oven. Add butter and brown on both sides. Cover with slices of salt pork. Add chicken broth, spices, celery, onion, and parsley. Cover the pan and roast in 350° oven 1½ hours. Remove birds to hot platter. Strain pan juices. Remove fat. Thicken with flour mixed with canned chicken broth to make gravy. Serves 6.

Brandied Breast of Pheasant

Remove bone from 6 breasts. Sprinkle with lemon juice, salt, and pepper. Brown in butter in heavy skillet or dutch oven. Cover, reduce heat, and cook slowly about 40 minutes or until done. Remove breasts. Cook 6 green onions, chopped fine, until limp. Slowly add 2 egg yolks and ¾ cup cream. Stir over low heat until blended. When thickened pour in 3 oz. brandy. Pour over pheasant. Use the leftover birds in Pheasant A La Queen or Pheasant Curry. Serves 6.

Mushroom Stuffed Breast of Pheasant

6 breasts with bone re- moved	crumbs
2 cups chopped mush- rooms	¼ cup cream
1½ tablespoons chopped onion	½ teaspoon salt
¼ cup dried bread	¼ teaspoon pepper
	2 eggs
	Cracker crumbs
	3 tablespoons butter

Make slit in each breast. Mix the mushrooms, onion, bread crumbs, cream, salt, and pepper. Stuff each breast. Roll in beaten eggs, then in cracker crumbs. Fry in butter until brown. Cover. Reduce heat and cook about 40 minutes or until done.

Serve with mushroom sauce made of 1 can (10½ oz.) mushroom soup thinned with ½ cup water and 5 tablespoons sherry wine. Serves 6.

French Herbed Pheasant

Cut up large pheasant in serving pieces. Coat with flour, salt, and freshly ground pepper. Brown in skillet in cooking oil. Remove pheasant. In same skillet add 8 small, whole onions, 8 small, peeled carrots, and 1 crushed garlic clove. Cover and cook 5 minutes.

In tea ball place 4 sprigs parsley, 1 bay leaf, ¼ teaspoon dried thyme, and 2-3 celery leaves. Place tea ball in large casserole. Add pheasant, vegetables, and 1 can (4 oz.) sliced mushrooms. Add 2 cups Burgundy wine. Cover. Bake in 350° oven 2 hours. Remove tea ball and serve. Serves 4.

Pheasant in Sour Cream Sauce

2 pheasants cut in serving pieces	1 stalk chopped celery
½ cup chopped onion	1 teaspoon salt
	4 peppercorns

Put wing tips, backs, and necks of pheasants in 2 cups water along with the above seasonings. Simmer 1 hour. Strain stock.

Dredge rest of pheasant pieces in seasoned flour. Heat 2 tablespoons butter in heavy skillet and brown pieces. Put in buttered casserole. Cook ½ cup diced onion, ½ cup diced celery, and 1 can (2 oz.) mushrooms in 2 tablespoons butter until soft. Sprinkle the vegetables over pheasant in casserole. Stir 4 tablespoons flour in the skillet. Gradually add 2 cups stock and 1 cup dry, white wine stirring constantly. Cook over low heat until thickened. Stir in 1 cup sour cream. Pour sauce over pheasant and bake covered in 350° oven 2 hours. Serves 6.

Pheasant with Sauerkraut

1 large trussed pheasant	4 crushed juniper berries
¼ cup brandy	1½ teaspoons caraway
1 teaspoon anchovy paste	seed
¼ cup melted butter	1 diced onion
1 can (27 oz.) sauerkraut	5 crushed peppercorns
½ cup Tokay wine	3 slices diced bacon

Pour brandy over pheasant. Let stand at least 3 hours. Mix paste into melted butter and pour over pheasant. Roast uncovered in 350° oven 1 hour or until browned.

Soak sauerkraut overnight in wine. Add juniper berries, caraway seed, onion, peppercorns, and bacon. Simmer 35 minutes. Place pheasant on bed of sauerkraut. Cover pan and bake in 350° oven 30 minutes.

Pheasant Fricassee

1 pheasant	¼ teaspoon thyme
½ cup flour	¼ teaspoon marjoram
1 teaspoon salt	1 cup broth or bouillon
¼ teaspoon pepper	1 cup cream
¼ cup cooking oil	

Cut pheasant into serving pieces. Dredge in flour mixed with salt, pepper, thyme, and marjoram. Brown in oil. Drain. Place in covered baking dish. Cover with broth and cream. Bake in 350° oven 1½ hours. Serves 4-6.

Roast Tokay Pheasant

1 trussed pheasant	cherry jelly
½ teaspoon salt	Tie in cheesecloth ball:
¼ teaspoon pepper	1 bay leaf
¼ cup melted butter	1 garlic clove
5 thin onion slices	1 whole clove
1 cup Tokay wine	2 tablespoons chopped
1 can (10½ oz.) chicken	celery leaves
gravy	1 slice chopped lemon
2 teaspoons currant or	

Place spice ball in bottom of dutch oven or covered roasting pan. Place pheasant in pan. Add salt, pepper, and melted butter over bird. Place onion slices on pheasant. Add wine and chicken gravy. Roast 1½ hours basting frequently. Remove to hot platter. Skim fat off pan drippings. Bring to boil and add 2 tablespoons currant or cherry jelly. Serve in gravy boat. Serves 4-6.

Southern Fried Pheasant

1 pheasant cut into	Batter:
serving pieces	2 eggs
½ teaspoon salt	½ cup milk
¼ teaspoon pepper	1 cup flour
2 cups shortening or	1 teaspoon baking
cooking oil	powder
	1 teaspoon salt
	1 teaspoon melted
	shortening

Cover pheasant pieces with water. Add salt and pepper and simmer for 1 hour or until tender. The pheasant may also be cooked in a pressure cooker 20-30 minutes or until tender. Remove from liquid and cool.

Sift flour, salt, and baking powder. Beat eggs, add milk, and shortening. Fold in flour but do not beat. Dip pheasant pieces in batter. Fry in hot shortening until golden brown. Serves 4-6.

Pheasant Curry

The following two recipes are an excellent way to use leftover pheasant.

3 cups diced, cooked pheasant	ginger
1 peeled, chopped apple	1 can (10½ oz.) chicken consommé
1 small, diced onion	1 cup milk
¼ cup butter	1 tablespoon lemon juice
1½ teaspoons curry powder	3 cups cooked rice
¼ cup flour	1 orange sliced thin
¼ teaspoon powdered	1 cup seedless grapes

Cook the onion and apple in butter in heavy pan until onion is limp. Sprinkle flour into pan. Add curry powder, salt, and ginger. Stir in the consommé and milk. Heat slowly and stir constantly. Add the pheasant and lemon juice. Simmer 5 minutes. Serve on hot rice and garnish with orange slices and grapes. Serves 4-6.

Pheasant A La Queen

3 cups cooked, diced pheasant	1 egg yolk
¼ cup butter	1 can (20 oz.) pineapple chunks
¼ cup flour	6 slices toast
1 teaspoon salt	¼ cup slivered almonds
2 cups milk	2 tablespoons butter

Melt butter. Stir in flour, salt, and milk. Cook over low heat until thickened. Pour a little sauce over the beaten egg yolk. Mix and stir back into the sauce. Add diced pheasant. Stir and heat. Add pineapple. Spoon on to hot toast. Brown almonds lightly in 2 tablespoons butter. Sprinkle on top of pheasant. Serves 6.

Grouse

Grouse have dark, lean, dry meat and should be

cooked in sauce or with butter, oil, bacon, or salt pork added. Like chicken, they should be thoroughly cooked. Some may have a gamey taste depending on their diet. To avoid this soak in a marinade 2-4 hours before cooking. The recipes for grouse and quail are interchangeable.

Broiled Grouse

After cleaning birds, soak in salt water for a few hours. Remove and wipe dry. Split the birds. Sprinkle with salt and brush with a mixture of melted butter and lemon juice. Place over glowing coals and broil 15 minutes on each side, or until done. Serve on toast with Cumberland Sauce on the side.

Roast Grouse in Wine

Stuff grouse if desired. Wrap with salt pork. Place in a covered roasting pan. Add 1 cup Marsala wine and roast in 300° oven 1-1½ hours or until done. Uncover for the last 20 minutes to brown. Remove birds. Thicken drippings in pan. Add water and season to taste. Cook slowly, stirring constantly until thickened.

Breast of Grouse

Remove breasts from 3-4 grouse. Reserve.

Grouse carcasses	**1 bay leaf**
1 piece diced salt pork	**2 tablespoons celery**
2 chopped onions	**leaves**
2 tablespoons chopped	**¼ cup chopped carrots**
parsley	**4 crushed peppercorns**
4 whole cloves	**Pinch marjoram**
2 crushed juniper berries	**½ cup claret wine**

Place carcasses of grouse in pressure cooker along with the rest of the ingredients. Cover with water and cook 30-40 minutes. Cool and skim off fat. Remove meat and skin from bones. Strain through sieve, pushing meat and vegetables through. Cook liquid until it is reduced to 1 cup.

Cook grouse breasts slowly in butter until golden brown. Add the strained meat and vegetables to liquid. Add ½ cup claret wine to meat sauce. Stir and place the browned grouse breasts on top. Cover and simmer slowly 20 minutes. Serve over rice. Serves 4.

Roast Grouse

Wipe birds, season with salt and pepper. Sprinkle with lemon juice. Wrap with slices of bacon. Wrap loosely in heavy-duty aluminum foil. Roast in 350° oven for 1-1½ hours. Remove birds. Skim fat from pan juices. Add 1 tablespoon butter and 1 can (10¾ oz.) beef gravy. Simmer until thickened and pour over grouse.

Grouse A La Cherie

4 grouse	½ cup port wine
1 teaspoon salt	1 can (10½ oz.) chicken
¼ teaspoon pepper	broth
2 tablespoons butter	¼ teaspoon cinnamon
½ cup chopped onion	2 whole cloves
½ cup chopped celery	2 tablespoons currant
1 tablespoon flour	jelly

Wipe grouse dry. Season with salt and pepper. Brown slowly in butter in heavy pan or dutch oven. Remove grouse. Add vegetables to pan and sauté until lightly brown. Sprinkle in flour. Add wine, chicken broth, cinnamon, and cloves. Stir over low heat until thickened. Return grouse to pan. Cover and simmer 30-40 minutes turning occasionally and adding water if needed. Remove grouse to hot platter. Stir jelly into sauce. Heat, stirring constantly until sauce is smooth. Season to taste and pour sauce over grouse. Serves 4.

Grouse With Wine

Cut 4 grouse into serving pieces. Mix 1½ cups Burgundy wine with 1 sliced onion, 1 bay leaf, 1 mashed garlic clove, 4 whole cloves, and 1 tablespoon brown sugar. Place pieces of grouse in deep bowl. Cover with the marinade and let stand in the refrigerator 1-2 days.

Remove birds and wipe dry. Dip in seasoned flour and brown slowly in hot oil. Strain the marinade. Place the birds and liquid into a casserole and cover. Bake in 300° oven 1-1½ hours. Remove birds to hot platter and pour remaining sauce over them. Serves 4.

Grouse Cutlets

This recipe is a delicious way for using leftover grouse, pheasant, or quail.

Chop 3-4 cups of leftover grouse or other game birds into tiny pieces. Mix with 3 cups soft bread crumbs. Add enough canned milk or cream to moisten. Stir in 2 tablespoons brandy. Season with salt and pepper. Blend in ½ cup melted butter and 3 egg yolks. Form into cutlets about ½ inch thick. Roll in fine bread crumbs. Fry in butter over medium heat. Serve with the following sauce:

Brown ¼ cup diced ham and 1 tablespoon chopped onion in butter. Add 1 can (10½ oz.) cream of chicken soup and ¼ cup Madeira wine. Heat and pour over cutlets. Serves 4-6.

Small Game

Rabbit
Squirrel
Opossum or Raccoon
Javelina (Peccary)

Rabbit

Rabbit is often overlooked as one of the best of small game animals. It is high in protein and lowest in calories of all meat. It is the largest, cheapest, and most available supply of game. Rabbit tastes much like chicken and may be fried, boiled, stewed, or used in any chicken casserole recipe. The cottontail is the most abundant and is best when taken during cold weather.

Young rabbits are usually tender, while old ones may be tough and stringy. A young rabbit is identifiable by the softness of its ears and paws. The rabbit should be skinned and dressed as soon as it is killed. The scent glands should be removed immediately or the meat will taste wild. These small nodules are under the front legs where they join the body. Keep the rabbit cool and soak in salt water for a few hours or overnight.

Fried Rabbit

Disjoint 1 rabbit into serving pieces. Soak in salt water overnight. Dredge in seasoned flour, and fry in hot fat over medium heat turning occasionally until brown. Add ½ cup water. Cover and steam 30 minutes or until tender. Serves 4.

Roast Rabbit

1-2 rabbits
½ cup Dijon (mild) mustard
½ cup melted butter
1 can (10½ oz.) cream of mushroom soup
1 cup half-half or canned milk
1 teaspoon salt
¼ teaspoon pepper
½ cup sherry

Cut rabbit into serving pieces. Coat each piece with Dijon mustard. Cover and let stand in refrigerator for several hours. Put in dutch oven. Cover with melted butter.

Cover and roast in 300° oven 1½ hours. Add mushroom soup, cream, salt, and pepper. Cook another 30 minutes. Remove rabbit to hot platter. Add sherry to pan drippings, stir, and simmer a few minutes. Pour over rabbit. Serves 4-6.

Hasenpfeffer

Dress and wash 2 rabbits. Cut in serving pieces and put in crock. Cover with vinegar and add 2 teaspoons salt, 1 teaspoon mixed spices, 1 tablespoon pepper, and 1 large, sliced onion. Cover and place in refrigerator 24 hours. Remove the meat. Cover with fresh water and simmer in heavy, covered pan 2 hours, or pressure cook 30 minutes. Reserve the broth. In a heavy skillet mix 2 tablespoons butter with 2 tablespoons flour. Add 1 tablespoon brown sugar. Stir over low heat until browned. Add 1 cup of broth and stir until thickened. Add the rabbit pieces and remaining broth. Add 1 teaspoon cinnamon, ½ teaspoon allspice, ¼ teaspoon cloves, 1 onion chopped fine, and 1 lemon sliced thin. Cover and simmer 30-40 minutes more adding liquid if needed. Serves 4-6.

Rabbit Stew

Cut rabbit into serving pieces. Place in heavy pot. Cover with water. Add 1 teaspoon salt, ½ teaspoon pepper, 1 minced garlic clove, and 1 bay leaf. Cover and simmer 1½-2 hours. Add 4 carrots cut into 2 inch pieces, 3 cubed potatoes, 2 diced onions, and ½ cup diced celery. Add 1 cup beer and simmer 30 minutes. The cooking time may be cut down by using a pressure cooker. Pressure the rabbit 35 minutes. Add vegetables and pressure 6 minutes. Be sure to add the beer because it gives a nutty flavor. Remove bay leaf. Serve rabbit pieces over vegetables. Serve broth on the side. Serves 4-6.

Squirrel

Squirrel meat is similar to rabbit but more delicate in flavor. The meat is very lean and some kind of fat, butter or bacon, should be added. Squirrels should be skinned and dressed immediately. Wash in several waters and soak in salt water several hours or overnight. Before cooking cover with salad oil mixed with the juice of 1 lemon and let stand for 1 hour or more.

Fried Squirrel

1 squirrel cut into serving pieces	¾ cup shortening
⅓ cup milk	½ cup flour
¼ teaspoon Tabasco sauce	1 teaspoon salt
	¼ teaspoon pepper

Place squirrel pieces in bowl. Add milk and Tabasco sauce. Let stand 1 hour or more in refrigerator. Mix flour with salt and pepper. Drain squirrel pieces and dredge in flour mixture. Heat shortening in skillet, add squirrel pieces and fry until golden brown. Cover, reduce heat, and continue cooking 30 minutes until done. Serves 4.

Roast Squirrel

3 small or 2 large squirrels	2 cups bread crumbs
½ cup cooking oil	½ cup milk
¼ cup lemon juice or vinegar	1 chopped onion
	1 teaspoon salt
	¼ teaspoon pepper

Cover squirrels with oil and vinegar in covered bowl. Let stand in refrigerator several hours or ovenight. Remove and drain. Toss bread crumbs with onion, salt, and pepper. Moisten with milk. Stuff the squirrels. Truss the forelegs back and the hindlegs forward. Baste with bacon fat. Roast uncovered in 325° oven 1½-2 hours basting frequently. When done make gravy with remaining drippings. Serves 6-8.

Brunswick Stew

2 squirrels cut into	serving pieces

1 tablespoon salt
1 chopped onion
2 cups dried lima beans
½ pound salt pork
6 ears or 2 cans corn
6 cubed potatoes

4 cups tomatoes
2 teaspoons sugar
1 teaspoon pepper
½ pound butter
2 tablespoons flour

Add salt to 4 quarts boiling water. Add squirrel pieces, onion, lima beans, and salt pork. Cover and simmer 3 hours or until beans are tender. Add corn, cut from the cob or canned corn, potatoes, tomatoes, sugar, and pepper, and simmer 30 minutes more. Cut butter into 1 inch pieces and roll in flour. Add to stew. Bring to boil and simmer until thickened. Serve in soup plates. Serves 6-8.

Opossum or Raccoon

The meat of these animals is very fat and greasy, and as much of the fat as possible should be trimmed off before cooking. As soon as the animal has been skinned, remove the musk glands to keep the meat from having a strong odor and taste. These small, reddish kernels are under the front legs and on both sides of the backbone near the rump. Dress out the animal and soak overnight in a salt or vinegar and water solution. Be sure the meat is cooked thoroughly.

Opossum Or Raccoon Roast

To dress, immerse in very hot water 1 minute. Remove and use dull knife to scrape off hair so that skin is not cut. Slit from bottom of throat to hind legs. Remove entrails. Remove head, tail, and lower legs. Wash thoroughly in hot water. Cover with cold water, add 1 cup salt and let stand overnight. Drain off water, rinse with boiling water. Stuff with bread stuffing or fruit stuffing, using apples and raisins. Sew up the carcass. Place in roasting pan. Add 1 cup water and baste occasionally. Most are very fat and need no additional larding. Test for doneness after 4 hours at 350°. When done remove carcass. Thicken juices in pan with cornstarch. Add salt and pepper and enough water to make a smooth gravy. Cook until thickened.

Javelina (Peccary)

Javelina weigh up to 50 pounds and taste much like pork. They feed primarily on prickly pear cactus, and the young pigs are very tender with fine-grained, light meat. Older ones may have a stronger flavor but may be soaked in soda or vinegar water, or in a marinade.

The animals have a peculiarly disagreeable odor which is caused by a musk sac on its back just forward of the hips. This sac must be removed as soon as the pig is killed. If this is done there is no wild or gamey taste. Chill the meat immediately.

When butchering the javelina, it is most convenient to skin out the pig because the hair is coarse. Soak the meat in a vinegar-water solution overnight. It is not necessary to hang or age the meat. Always make sure the meat is well cooked.

Whole Roast Javelina

Dig a pit about 3 feet around and at least 2 feet deep. Line with rocks. Build a hot charcoal fire on top of the rocks. Use plenty of charcoal.

Prepare javelina by scrubbing entire carcass with stiff brush. Close the eyes and curl the tail. Season with salt and pepper. Brush all over with a mixture of melted butter and lemon juice. Cover the whole pig with a heavy flour and water paste, or wrap securely in heavy-duty aluminum foil. Place pig on hot coals. Cover pit with about 6 inches of dirt and roast 8-12 hours depending on the size of the pig. Check the heat occasionally and add more charcoal. If you have used paste, peel off crust and discard.

Serve with the proverbial apple in the mouth. Serves 10-12.

Roast Javelina Ham

Cut ham from upper leg of javelina. Cut off all fat. Mix 1 cup melted butter, 1 teaspoon salt, ¾ cup brown sugar, and 1 tablespoon mustard. Coat ham on all sides with this mixture. Place in a shallow, uncovered, roasting pan, and roast in 325° oven 3½ hours or more. Baste about every 15 minutes with apple cider. Pour off fat and make a gravy with the drippings, adding a can (10½ oz.) bouillion for the liquid. Serves 6.

Javelina Chops

Since the javelina is much smaller than the domestic pig, the chops are also smaller so allow 2-3 chops per person.

Remove all fat from 8-10 chops. Rub chops with a cut garlic clove. Brown slowly in cooking oil. Add 1 can (10½ oz.) chicken consommé. Cover and simmer 40 minutes or until done. Serves 4.

Large Game

Deer
Antelope
Elk
Barbary Sheep
Bear
Buffalo

Deer

Much venison is found unpalatable at the table because proper precautions were not taken in the field by the hunter. For detailed instructions on field dressing see Field Dressing section.

Venison resembles beef or veal in flavor, texture, color, and general characteristics. The flavor is gamey but not strong. If you find this taste objectionable much of it can be removed by soaking the meat in milk for an hour or more. Venison is lean, fine textured, and tends to be a little dry. It should have suet, bacon, butter, salt pork, or other fat added. Venison stays quite pink even when well done, so caution should be used not to overcook it, making it dry and unflavorful.

Roast Saddle of Venison

Marinade:
½ cup honey
½ cup tomato sauce
½ cup bourbon
1 crushed garlic clove
¼ teaspoon powdered
  ginger
¼ cup soy sauce

4-5 slices salt pork
2 tablespoons flour
½ cup sour cream
½ cup red wine

Mix marinade. Pour over 6-8 pound saddle of venison and marinate in refrigerator 12-24 hours turning occasionally. Remove venison and put in shallow roasting pan. Cover with salt pork. Roast in 325° oven 3-4 hours basting often with marinade. Discard pork. Remove roast to hot platter. Blend flour with sour cream. Add to strained sauce in pan. Heat, stirring constantly until thickened. Add wine and season to taste. Serves 6-8.

Venison Filet Mignon

Allow 2-3 filets per person. Wrap bacon around filets and fasten with a toothpick. Sprinkle with garlic salt and freshly ground pepper. Cook 8-10 minutes on each side in an electric skillet. Reduce heat and add 1 cup Sauterne wine. Cook slowly to desired doneness.

Venison Steaks or Chops

Marinade No. 1:	**Marinade No. 2:**
2 cups vinegar	**2 cups red wine**
2 cups red wine	**½ cup olive oil**
1 sliced lemon	**1½ cups chopped celery**
1 tablespoon crushed	**1 garlic clove**
juniper berries	**2 whole cloves**
1 teaspoon pepper	**1 stick cinnamon**

Marinate steaks or chops 12-24 hours. Remove and drain. Heat heavy skillet with ½ cup cooking oil and ¼ cup butter. Sauté meat turning frequently until browned. Salt and pepper to taste. Baste often with the marinade. Cover and simmer 20-30 minutes.

Venison Chops Polonaise

Cover 6 thick chops with instant or homemade marinade. Remove chops and sauté in 4 tablespoons butter 15 minutes or until browned on both sides. Add ½ cup marinade. Simmer slowly 30-40 minutes. Remove chops. Slowly stir in 1 cup sour cream and ¼ cup Parmesan cheese. Heat and pour sauce over chops. Serves 4.

Lumberjack Cutlets

Marinade:	**1 bay leaf**
½ cup oil	**1 crushed garlic clove**
Juice of 1 lemon	**1 teaspoon salt**
4 ground peppercorns	
1 tablespoon parsley	

Use 2 pounded loin steaks or deboned rib or round steaks per person. Let meat stand in marinade 4-6 hours or longer. Remove and place in baking dish. Pour the marinade and ¼ cup sherry wine over meat. Bake in 350° oven 30 minutes or until done. Place on heated platter. Thicken drippings. Add water if needed. Add 1 tablespoon gin and 1 tablespoon horseradish. Serve with chops. Serves 4-6.

Venison Swiss Steak

Mix ½ cup flour with 1 teaspoon salt and ¼ teaspoon pepper. Pound seasoned flour into a 3-4 pound round or Swiss steak. Heat 2 tablespoons shortening in heavy skillet or dutch oven, and brown meat on both sides. Add 3 sliced onions, 1 can (29 oz.) tomatoes, 1½ tablespoons Worcestershire sauce, 1 cup Burgundy wine, 1 whole clove, and ½ crushed garlic clove. Cover pot. Bake in 350° oven 2½ hours, adding water if necessary, until fork tender. Serves 6.

Sukiyaki

Be very careful not to overcook the vegetables as they should be crispy. Serve with hot fluffy rice and tea.

2 pounds steak, cut in thin diagonal slices, 2 inches wide, ½ inch thick	1 can (8½ oz.) bamboo shoots sliced thin
2 tablespoons cooking oil	1 can (4 oz.) sliced mushrooms and juice
2 tablespoons sugar	1 bunch green onions cut in ½ inch lengths with tops
¾ cup soy sauce	
2 thinly sliced onions	1 bunch fresh green spinach or 1 package (12 oz.) frozen
1½ cups celery, sliced diagonally in 1 inch strips	

Heat oil in skillet. Add meat and brown lightly. Mix sugar, soy sauce, and mushroom juice. Add half of this mixture to the meat. Push meat to one side of the pan and add sliced onions and celery. Cook 5 minutes. Add remaining soy sauce mixture, bamboo shoots, mushrooms, and green onions. Cover with well washed spinach leaves and steam until spinach is limp, about 10 minutes. Serves 8.

Venison Shish Kebabs

Marinade:	**1 minced garlic clove**
1 cup red wine	**½ cup olive oil**

2 pounds steak,	**2 green peppers cut in 1**
cut in 1½ inch cubes	**inch squares**
½ teaspoon salt	**2 white onions cut in 1**
¼ teaspoon pepper	**inch squares**
½ pound bacon	

Place meat in marinade 4-6 hours. Remove and drain. Thread slice of bacon on skewer. Add cube of meat, 1 onion piece, and 1 green pepper piece. Pull bacon up and thread on skewer. Continue until piece measures about 5-6 inches on skewer. Sprinkle with salt and pepper. Brush with marinade. Broil over hot coals turning often and basting with marinade. Cook to desired doneness. Serves 6.

Pot Roast of Venison

Use a 3-4 pound roast. Rub with ½ cup flour mixed with 1 tablespoon salt and ¼ teaspoon pepper. Brown meat in 2 tablespoons shortening in dutch oven. Turn often because any burned flour will ruin the taste. Place a low rack under the meat. Add 1 cup water, ½ sliced onion, 3 whole peppercorns, and 1 bay leaf. Cover and simmer slowly 2½-3 hours or until fork tender. Turn once or twice during cooking period and add more water to keep ½-1 inch of water in the bottom of the pan. Serves 4-6.

Savory Pot Roast

3-4 pound roast	**¼ teaspoon pepper**
¼ cup fat	**¼ teaspoon ginger**
2 sliced onions	**4 whole cloves**
1 can (6 oz.) tomato paste	**6 peeled, quartered**
1 cup water	**potatoes**
1 teaspoon salt	**6 scraped, halved carrots**

Brown meat in fat in heavy pan or dutch oven. Slip low rack under the meat. Add the onions, tomato paste, water, and seasonings. Cover tightly and simmer over low heat or bake in 350° oven 3 hours adding water if needed. Add the potatoes and carrots, and cook 30-40 minutes longer. Serves 4-6.

Venison Cutlets

Trim 6 cutlets of all fat and rub with salt and pepper. Dip in flour. Brown in hot skillet in cooking oil or bacon grease. Add ½ cup cream. Simmer until tender. Place on hot platter and cover with melted butter. Serves 3-4.

Barbecued Venison Steaks

4-6 boneless steaks	1 teaspoon salt
1 crushed garlic clove	¼ teaspoon pepper
¼ cup oil	1 teaspoon dry mustard
¼ cup melted butter	2 teaspoons lemon juice

Combine garlic, oil, butter, salt, pepper, mustard, and lemon juice. Let stand 30 minutes. Start charcoal fire about 45 minutes ahead. Broil steaks, turning occasionally and basting with sauce. Cook to desired doneness. Serves 4-6.

Oriental Steak

2 pounds steak	2 cups diagonally sliced celery
Meat tenderizer	
1 tablespoon steak sauce	1 package (6 oz.) frozen peas
1 teaspoon salt	
2 tablespoons soy sauce	1 tablespoon cornstarch
1 can (10½ oz.) beef consommé	2 tablespoons water
	2 small tomatoes
1 large onion cut in rings	

Put meat tenderizer on steak. Cut across grain in strips. Brown in oil with steak sauce. Add salt, soy sauce, and consommé. Simmer covered 15 minutes. Lay onion rings and celery on steak. Cook 5 minutes. Add peas and cook 3 minutes. Blend corn starch in water and stir into meat mixture. Add tomatoes cut into wedges. Heat and serve with parsleyed rice. Serves 4-6.

Venison and Apple Birds

1½ pounds boneless steak	¼ cup seedless raisins
⅓ cup flour	¼ cup chopped celery
1 teaspoon salt	1 cup chopped apples
¼ teaspoon pepper	1 teaspoon dry mustard
1 cup fresh bread crumbs	¼ teaspoon sage
	1 cup apple juice

Pound flour, salt, and pepper into steak. Cut into 5-6 rounds (4-5 inches round and ¼ inch thick). Mix stuffing. Place mound of stuffing on each steak. Roll up and fasten with toothpick. Brown rolls in oil. Add apple juice. Cover and simmer 1 hour adding water if needed. Serves 4.

Peppercorn Steak

1½ pounds boneless steak	1 tablespoon oil
1 tablespoon whole peppercorns	⅓ cup white wine
	Pimiento
	Parsley

Crush peppercorns in cloth with rolling pin. Press into steak. Let stand 30 minutes. Heat oil in heavy skillet. Brown steak turning often. Add wine and simmer until done. Garnish with pimiento and parsley. Serves 4.

Stuffed Venison Steak

4-6 steaks ¼ inch thick	mary, and thyme
½ cup flour	1 can (10½ oz.) beef bouillon
1 teaspoon salt	1½ cups sage dressing
¼ teaspoon pepper	
Pinch of marjoram, rose-	

Pound flour, salt, and pepper well into each steak. Place a mound of dressing on each one. Fold meat over and fasten with a toothpick. Place in baking dish. Add bouillon and herbs. Bake in 350° oven 1 hour or until fork tender. Serves 4.

Venison Scaloppine

6-8 very thin boneless
　steaks
½ cup flour
4 tablespoons cooking oil
½ teaspoon salt
½ teaspoon freshly

ground pepper
¼ teaspoon marjoram
¼ teaspoon rosemary
1 can (10½ oz.) beef
　consommé
½ cup Marsala wine

Lightly coat steaks in flour mixed with salt and pepper. Brown slowly on both sides in oil. Remove meat. Stir in consommé, herbs, and wine. Return meat to pan and simmer over low heat 20 minutes. Serve over rice or buttered spaghetti. Serves 4.

Epicurean Venison

2 pounds steak cut in
　narrow strips
½ cup flour
1 teaspoon salt
¼ teaspoon pepper
¼ teaspoon each rose-
　mary, thyme, and
　savory
3 tablespoons flour

1 can (14 oz.) chicken
　broth
1 can (10½ oz.) cream of
　mushroom soup
1 can (10½ oz.) cream of
　chicken soup
1 cup white wine
3 tablespoons cooking oil

Coat steak strips with mixture of flour, salt, pepper, and herbs. Place in heavy skillet with oil. Brown slowly on all sides. Remove meat and place in baking dish. Add the 3 tablespoons flour to drippings in skillet. Stir and add the remaining ingredients. Simmer. Pour over meat. Cover with buttered bread crumbs and bake in 350° oven 1 hour. Serve with wild or browned rice. Serves 6.

Italian Steak

Sauce:
1 can (15 oz.) spaghetti
　sauce
3 tablespoons vinegar
1 small, chopped onion

1 teaspoon salt
¼ teaspoon pepper
1 teaspoon Worcester-
　shire sauce

2 pounds round steak	**1½ inches thick**

Mix sauce ingredients and bring to boil. Reduce heat and simmer 15 minutes. Cool. Cover steak with sauce and marinate overnight. Drain. Place steak on hot coals and grill 8-10 minutes on each side or to desired doneness. Baste often with sauce. Cut on the bias and serve with hot buttered spaghetti or any pasta. Serves 6.

Herbed Venison Roast

1 shoulder or rump roast	**½ teaspoon grated**
Instant marinade	**orange rind**
6-8 whole cloves	**¼ teaspoon pepper**
½ cup brown sugar	**Pinch thyme and rose-**
½ teaspoon garlic salt	**mary**

Sprinkle all sides of roast with instant marinade. Mix the brown sugar, garlic salt, orange rind, pepper, and spices, and cover the top of the roast. Stick cloves into the meat. Roast in 450° oven 30 minutes. Reduce heat to 325° and roast 2 hours more or to desired doneness. Remove to hot platter. Skim fat from juices in pan. Thicken with 2 tablespoons flour and 1½ cups water. Season to taste. Stir until thickened. Serve gravy on side with roast. Serves 6-8.

Venison Tereyaki

2 pounds filet cut in	**½ cup soy sauce**
½ inch strips	**½ cup sherry wine**
1 envelope onion soup	**2 tablespoons brown**
mix	**sugar**

Combine soup mix, soy sauce, sherry, and brown sugar. Thread meat on skewers and marinate 3-4 hours in mixture. Grill over hot coals turning often and basting with sauce. Heat remaining sauce and pour over steaks. Serves 4-6.

Braised Port Venison Roast

4-6 pound roast	**1 cup port wine**

1 pound suet	**1 tablespoon butter**
½ teaspoon salt	**1 tablespoon water**
½ teaspoon pepper	**1 tablespoon flour**
¼ teaspoon allspice	

Soak suet in wine 2 hours. Sprinkle roast with salt, pepper, and allspice. Wrap suet around roast. Tie with string. Pour wine over roast. Mix butter with flour in a roux. Stir in water and pour over roast. Cook covered over low heat 3-4 hours or until tender adding more water as needed. Untie suet and discard. Serves 6-8.

Jellied Venison in Port

Soak a 4-6 pound leg of venison in salt water 2 hours. Remove and sprinkle with instant marinade. Add 1 large beef soup bone. Cover with water and simmer 4-6 hours or until meat falls from bone. Remove meat and force into large square mold. Meanwhile cook stock down to 1 cup. Add ½ cup port wine and heat. Pour stock over meat and set in refrigerator to chill 3-4 hours. Unmold on platter and decorate with hard-boiled egg slices and watercress. Serves 6-8.

South Seas Venison Steaks

4-6 steaks	**½ green pepper cut in**
Unseasoned meat	**strips**
tenderizer	**3 stalks celery cut in**
½ teaspoon salt	**diagonal strips**
¼ teaspoon pepper	**3 ounces shredded**
1 cup dry vermouth	**coconut**
1½ cups rice	**½ teaspoon nutmeg**
1 small, chopped onion	**2 cups water**

Sprinkle steaks with meat tenderizer, salt, and pepper. Put in roasting pan. Cover with vermouth. Bake in 325° oven 1 hour. Add rice, onion, pepper, celery, coconut, nutmeg, and water. Cover pan and return to oven 30-40 minutes. Serves 4.

Sherry Chops

Marinade:	**6-8 chops**
1 chopped onion	**½ teaspoon salt**
1 crushed garlic clove	**¼ teaspoon pepper**
1½ teaspoons dry mustard	
1½ tablespoons melted butter	
1½ cups sherry wine	

Pour marinade over chops and place in refrigerator for at least 4 hours. Drain chops and place on grill over hot coals. Season with salt and pepper. Strain marinade and baste chops as they cook turning often. Heat remaining marinade and pour over chops when done. Serves 6.

Venison Liver

Soak liver in salt water 3-4 hours. Remove and drain. Cut into thin slices. Dredge in seasoned flour and brown quickly in bacon grease. Remove liver. Add 1 large, sliced, Bermuda onion. Cook until limp and serve over liver.

Venison Heart

Another delicacy from a venison hunt is the heart. Squeeze in several waters to remove blood. Remove outer skin and membranes. Chop very fine and fry in bacon grease. Add eggs and scramble. Great for breakfast.

Venison Pâté

A very different and delicious cold loaf. Nice to serve at buffet parties.

½ pound boneless venison	**½ teaspoon ginger**
¼ pound cooked tongue	**¼ teaspoon cinnamon**
¼ pound raw liver	**¼ teaspoon cloves**
1 onion	**½ teaspoon garlic salt**
1 egg	**¼ teaspoon thyme and rosemary**
1 teaspoon dry mustard	**½ teaspoon Knox gelatin**

Grind the venison, tongue, liver, and onion together twice. Beat egg and mix with meat. Add spices and mix well. Place in loaf pan. Cover and bake in 350° oven 1 hour. Remove. Place on platter. Dissolve gelatin in 1 tablespoon lukewarm water and spoon over pâté. Chill several hours. Decorate with sliced olives and sliced hard boiled egg.

Antelope

Much of the Western United States is fortunate in having what many hunters consider the most delicious of any wild game, the colorful antelope. Because of game management requirements antelope hunts are held in hot weather, usually August or September. The animal must be bled as soon as it is killed. The hide must be removed promptly, and the meat chilled. Many hunters take ice along on an antelope hunt for this purpose. A single animal usually dresses out from 60 to 100 pounds of meat.

Almost without exception, the meat is extremely tender and savory without the strong flavor of other wild game so that a marinade is not required. It may be cooked much as veal. Rubbing the meat with lemon juice enhances the flavor.

Whole Antelope Loin Roast

Leave one loin whole when butchering antelope. Thread on spit. Brush whole with lime juice mixed with melted butter, salt, pepper, and 2 minced garlic cloves.

Place seasoned loin over large bed of glowing coals. If using a barbecue pit without a spit turn the meat often. Baste frequently with lime juice mixture. Test for doneness after about 3 hours. If you like part of it rare, this should be about long enough. Serve with rice and a mushroom sauce. Serves 15.

Antelope Steaks with Bacon

Debone steaks or use filets. Wrap with bacon and secure with a toothpick. Sprinkle with garlic salt and freshly ground pepper. If you question the tenderness, sprinkle with unseasoned meat tenderizer. Fry in an electric skillet or over glowing coals on a barbecue pit. When done, turn down heat, or if using barbecue pit, remove to pan. Place over low heat. Add ½ cup port wine and simmer slowly 10 minutes. Allow 1 large or 2 small filets per person.

Antelope Steaks with Sherry

4-6 steaks	3 tablespoons shortening
1 teaspoon salt	⅓ cup water
¼ teaspoon pepper	¼ cup sherry
¼ cup flour	1 can (11 oz.) mushroom
1 lemon	sauce

Rub the antelope steaks with lemon juice. Season with salt and pepper. Dredge in flour. Brown in hot fat in skillet. Reduce heat. Add water, cover, and simmer until tender. Add the mushroom sauce and sherry. Simmer 5 minutes. Serve over rice or hot buttered noodles. Serves 4-6.

Parmesan Antelope Chops

6-8 chops	3 tablespoons shortening
1 lemon	1 can (10½ oz.) cream of
1 teaspoon salt	celery soup
¼ teaspoon pepper	¼ cup Parmesan cheese

Rub the antelope chops with lemon juice and sprinkle with salt and pepper. Brown in hot fat in skillet. Transfer to baking pan. Cover with celery soup and Parmesan cheese. Bake in 350° oven 30 minutes. Serves 6-8.

Anteham Rolls

6-8 boneless steaks cut	in thin slices

¼ pound butter	1 package cheese sauce
6-8 slices thinly sliced	mix
ham	Parmesan cheese

Beat pieces of antelope steak out as thin as possible. Place a pat of butter on each piece. Put a piece of thinly sliced ham on top. Roll and fasten with a toothpick. Brown in butter in skillet on all sides. Remove toothpicks. Fix cheese sauce mix as directed on package. Cover meat with cheese sauce. Sprinkle with Parmesan cheese and put under broiler until bubbly. Serves 4-6.

Antelope Cutlets in Sour Cream

6-8 cutlets	Flour
1 lemon	1 egg well beaten
1 teaspoon salt	Cracker crumbs
½ teaspoon pepper	½ pint sour cream

Pound cutlets until about ¼ inch thick. Rub with juice of lemon. Season with salt and pepper. Dip in flour, then in the beaten egg, and then in the cracker crumbs. Chill in refrigerator 1 hour. Brown cutlets in hot fat in skillet. Reduce heat and add sour cream. Cover and simmer until tender. Serves 6-8.

Antlope Roast

4-6 pound loin or leg	½ teaspoon salt
roast	¼ teaspoon pepper
1 lemon	1 garlic clove
4 slices salt pork or bacon	

Rub the roast with lemon juice. Season with salt and pepper. Insert slivers of garlic into the roast. Place slices of salt pork or bacon across the roast. Place on a rack in an uncovered pan. Bake in 300° oven 30 minutes per pound or to 180° on a meat thermometer. Serve with hot brown gravy mix. Serves 6-8.

Pot Roast of Antelope

4-6 pound shoulder or	rump roast

Juice of 1 lemon
1 teaspoon salt
¼ teaspoon pepper
¼ cup flour
1½ cups water
4 whole peppercorns

1 garlic clove
2 bay leaves
6-8 small onions
8-10 small, peeled
   potatoes
2 tablespoons shortening

Rub the roast with lemon juice. Dredge in flour, salt, and pepper. Melt the shortening in heavy covered skillet or dutch oven. Brown meat on all sides. Add the spices and water. Reduce heat. Cover and simmer about 2½ hours adding more water as needed. Place the onions and potatoes around the meat and simmer another 30-40 minutes. Remove the meat and vegetables to a hot platter. Strain the remaining liquid in the pan and reserve. Melt 2 tablespoons butter in the pan. Stir in 2 tablespoons flour. Mix thoroughly. Add the strained liquid and more water if needed to make a smooth gravy. Season to taste. Serves 6-8.

Barbecued Antelope Ribs

6-8 pounds ribs
1 lemon
1 teaspoon salt
½ teaspoon pepper
1 bottle prepared
   barbecue sauce
      or

Homemade Barbecue
   Sauce:
½ cup diced onion
¼ cup diced celery
1½ cups tomato catsup
2 tablespoons brown
   sugar
2 tablespoons Worcester-
   shire sauce
2 tablespoons vinegar
Simmer 30 minutes.

On Outdoor Grill:

Rub ribs with lemon juice. Sprinkle with salt and pepper. Place on grill over glowing coals. Raise grill until ribs are 1½ inches from coals. Turn occasionally basting with barbecue sauce 30-40 minutes or until done.

On Spit:

Rub ribs with lemon juice. Sprinkle with salt and

pepper. Thread onto spit. Place over bed of red-hot coals. Rotate ribs on spit 30-40 minutes basting often with barbecue sauce. Serves 4-6.

Antelope Burger

With any wild game most of the tough parts (neck, back, lower leg, etc.) are best ground into burger. Most meat shops or processing plants will grind this for you, or you can grind your own. Add about ⅓ suet as the meat is very lean.

Antelope burger is best mixed with part hamburger and/or sausage for meat loaf or meatballs.

Mix with chopped onions, bread crumbs, salt, pepper, garlic, and 1 beaten egg. Make into meat loaf or roll into balls. Cook until well done.

Antelope Liver

Antelope liver is comparable to veal liver and is best when simply floured, seasoned, and browned slowly in hot fat. Avoid overcooking. It is excellent cooked with bacon or sliced onions. Serves 4-6.

Baked Stuffed Antelope Heart

Skin heart and remove valves. Cut down about ¾ way. Make Bread Stuffing. Pack into cavity. Add salt and pepper. Pour ½ cup melted butter over heart. Place in a covered dutch oven with 1 cup of water. Bake in 350° oven 1½ hours. Serves 4.

Boiled Antelope Tongue

Remove membrane from tongue. Soak in cold salt water 3-4 hours. Drain. Cover with water, 1 garlic clove, 1 onion, 1 carrot, and 3 peppercorns. Simmer gently 2-3 hours. Remove from liquid. Chill. Serve sliced thinly. Serves 2-4.

Elk

Elk season is held during cold weather, and the animals usually remain in high, snowy country so there is less chance of meat spoilage than with other animals. Most elk meat is tender and has a more subtle flavor than venison which is more gamey. The meat is more coarse than venison, especially in the older animals.

As in all wild game, all the fat must be trimmed away. The steaks are more tender when soaked in a marinade; this will also accent the flavor of the roasts. Large roasts are delicious corned, sliced thin, and served either hot or cold. Most beef or venison recipes may be used for elk, as well as any of the recipes for ground meat and stew meat. Elk is excellent processed into lunch meat or sausage.

Roast Elk

Marinade:	**10 whole peppercorns**
3 garlic cloves	**2 teaspoons salt**
3 stalks diced celery	**2 sliced onions**
2 bay leaves	**½ cup vinegar**
10 juniper berries	**1 cup red wine**

Mix all ingredients. There are some instant marinades on the market that are very good and much faster.

5-6 pound roast	**12 small, peeled, whole**
4 tablespoons shortening	**onions**
6 carrots peeled and	**1 tablespoon chopped**
halved	**parsley**

Place roast in large bowl. Cover with marinade and allow to stand in the refrigerator 1-2 days turning occasionally. Remove roast. Strain marinade discarding spices and solids. Heat shortening in heavy pot and brown roast on both sides. Add 1 cup of the strained marinade. Cover and simmer 3-4 hours or until tender adding more water if needed. Add carrots and cook 30 minutes more. Add onions and cook until tender. Remove to hot platter. Skim fat from pan juices. Add remaining marinade and cook until it is reduced by ⅓. Thicken with a roux of flour and butter. Stir until smooth and thickened. Serve sauce separately. Serves 8-10.

Elk Filets

6 filets	1 teaspoon Worcester-
1 teaspoon salt	shire sauce
½ teaspoon pepper	½ cup red wine
10-12 slices bacon	

Wrap bacon around filets and secure with a toothpick. Sprinkle with salt and pepper. Grill over hot coals. Elk is very lean and will be more tender if cooked to rare or medium doneness. Remove to pan. Add Worcestershire sauce and wine, and simmer a few minutes. Pour pan juices over steaks. Serves 6.

Baked Elk Chops

6-8 chops	1 can (17 oz.) cream
4 tablespoons cooking oil	style corn
1 teaspoon salt	1 can (5⅓ oz.)
½ teaspoon pepper	evaporated milk
1 silced onion	Bread crumbs
1 sliced green pepper	2 tablespoons butter

Season chops with salt and pepper. Brown in hot cooking oil on both sides in heavy skillet. Put chops in a baking dish or casserole. Place onion and green pepper on top of the chops. Cover with corn and canned milk. Sprinkle with bread crumbs and dot with butter. Bake in 350° oven 1 hour or until tender. Serves 6.

Braised Elk Steak

6-8 steaks	½ teaspoon pepper
½ cup flour	¼ teaspoon garlic salt
1 teaspoon salt	4 tablespoons cooking oil

1 can (11 oz.) mushroom sauce or gravy	½ cup sherry wine

Mix flour, salt, pepper, and garlic salt. Pound into steaks. Brown in heavy skillet in cooking oil. Add mushroom sauce or gravy and wine. Simmer, covered, 1 hour or until tender. Serves 6-8.

Green Pepper Elk Steak

1½ pounds steak	3 green peppers cut into
2 sliced onions	strips
1 teaspoon thyme	½ cup red wine
1 cup bouillon	1 teaspoon Worcester-
1 teaspoon salt	shire sauce
¼ teaspoon pepper	3 tablespoons cooking oil

Cut meat into four steaks. Brown in hot fat in heavy skillet. Add onions, thyme, bouillon, salt, and pepper. Cover and simmer 1 hour or until tender. Add green peppers, wine, and Worcestershire sauce and simmer 20 minutes more. Serves 4.

Elk Sauerbraten

Marinade:	4-5 pound roast
2 cups vinegar	⅓ cup flour
2½ cups water	3 tablespoons cooking oil
2 sliced onions	6 ginger snaps
1 sliced lemon	3 tablespoons flour
1 tablespoon salt	2 tablespoons butter
3 tablespoons sugar	
8 whole cloves	
4 bay leaves	
6 whole peppercorns	

Place meat in large bowl. Combine marinade ingredients and pour over meat. Cover and allow to stand in refrigerator 1-2 days. Turn meat occasionally.

Remove meat from mixture. Coat with flour. Heat oil in a heavy skillet and brown meat on all sides.

Strain the marinade and discard the spices. Add

1 cup of the marinade to the meat. Cover and cook slowly on top of stove or in 350° oven 3 hours or until tender. Add more liquid as needed.

To make German gravy, strain fat from pan drippings. Blend in butter and flour. Add crumbled ginger snaps and remaining marinade. Stir until thickened and season to taste. Serves 6-8.

Tropical Elk Steak

Marinade:
1 minced garlic clove
½ teaspoon thyme
½ teaspoon mace
½ teaspoon nutmeg
2 tablespoons chopped
  parsley
2 sliced onions
1 teaspoon salt
½ teaspoon pepper
Few drops angostura
  bitters
¼ cup dark rum

3 pounds round steak
  (1½ inches thick)
4 tablespoons butter

Mix marinade ingredients. Place round steak in bowl and cover with marinade. Place in refrigerator at least 4 hours. Remove. Place meat in heavy skillet and brown slowly in butter. Add ½ cup water to the marinade and pour over the steak. Cover and simmer or bake in 350° oven 2 hours. Serves 6.

Piñon Elk Steak

8-10 steaks
  (5 inches round by
  ¼ inch)
⅓ cup flour
1 teaspoon salt
¼ teaspoon thyme
3 tablespoons shortening

¼ teaspoon pepper
½ cup piñon nuts
½ cup bread crumbs
2 tablespoons melted
  butter
1 can (10½ oz.) beef
  consommé

Mix flour, thyme, salt, and pepper. Pound into

steaks. Brown slowly in hot shortening. Remove from pan.

Mix nuts, bread crumbs, and melted butter. Spread 1 rounded tablespoon of mixture on 4-5 steaks. Cover with remaining steaks and secure edges with toothpicks. Place steaks in baking dish and cover with consommé. Bake, covered, in 300° oven 45 minutes adding more water if needed. Remove toothpicks. Pour remaining sauce over steaks. Serves 4-5.

Elk Paprika

2 pounds round steak	1 beef bouillon cube
2 tablespoons fat	1 tablespoon Worcester-
1 teaspoon salt	shire sauce
1 teaspoon paprika	½ pint sour cream
1 minced garlic clove	2 tablespoons flour
1 cup boiling water	1 teaspoon paprika

Rub the meat with salt and paprika. Melt fat in heavy skillet. Add the garlic and brown slowly. Brown the meat on both sides. Melt the bouillon cube in hot water. Add this and the Worcestershire sauce to the meat. Cover and cook slowly about 2 hours or until tender adding more water as needed. Add sour cream and remaining teaspoon of paprika. Simmer slowly for a few minutes. Remove the steak. Thicken broth with the 2 tablespoons flour mixed with ½ cup cold water. Stir until smooth and thickened. Serve the gravy over the meat. Serves 4-6.

Savory Elk

3-4 pound roast	cloves
3 large, sliced onions	½ teaspoon savory
3 tablespoons fat	2 cups boiling water
3 tablespoons flour	1 bouillon cube
1 teaspoon salt	2 tablespoons vinegar
¼ teaspoon pepper	2 tablespoons catsup
¼ teaspoon ground	

Brown onions in fat. Remove. Cut the meat into serving pieces. Mix flour and seasonings. Roll meat pieces in seasoned flour. Brown meat on all sides. Add bouillon cube to boiling water. Stir until dissolved. Return onions to pan. Add the bouillon. Slowly stir in vinegar and catsup. Cover and simmer 2 hours or until tender. Serves 6-8.

Corned Elk

Use a large crock or plastic tub. Place large roast in container. Cover with cold water. Let stand in refrigerator 48 hours. Drain.

For every 1 gallon of water add 1½ pounds of salt, ½ pound brown sugar, and ½ ounce saltpeter. Boil mixture and cool. Cover meat with corning liquid. Place a heavy weight on meat to keep it under the brine. Place in the refrigerator. It will be ready to use after 10 days. The corned meat may then be frozen or cooked.

Boiled Corned Elk

6 pounds corned meat	celery leaves
1 diced carrot	1 teaspoon chopped
1 chopped onion	parsley
8-10 whole peppercorns	Vinegar
1 teaspoon chopped	

Remove meat from corning liquid. Cover with water. Let stand 1 hour. Drain. Place in large kettle. Add carrot, onion, peppercorns, celery leaves, and parsley. Cover with water. Add 1 teaspoon vinegar for each quart of water. Simmer about 40 minutes per pound or until tender. You may cook in a pressure cooker 30-40 minutes. Remove and serve with boiled cabbage or allow to cool and slice thin.

Barbary Sheep

Barbary sheep are African imports and though less than fifty permits to hunt them were issued in 1971, they are now on the increase and more permits will be issued each year. For the most part the meat from young rams or ewes is edible, but the older ram meat is tough. The meat resembles antelope more than any other wild game, perhaps a little less tender and more dry, but with no discernable wild taste or cooking odor as in other sheep.

Barbary Barbecued Ribs

Allow ½ to 1 pound ribs per person. The sheep needs no marinade or soaking as there is no wild taste.

Pressure-cook a rack of ribs 15-20 minutes in salted water. Remove from liquid. Trim off all tallow.

Melt 3 tablespoons cooking oil in frying pan. Add ½ cup finely chopped onion, 1 chopped garlic clove, and cook until golden. Add 1½ cups catsup, 2 tablespoons brown sugar, 2 tablespoons Worcestershire sauce, and ¼ cup dry wine. Simmer 15-20 minutes.

Arrange ribs over hot coals on barbecue grill. Brush generously with sauce. Turn frequently and baste often about 15-20 minutes. You will have delicious barbecue this way in less than an hour. Place on heated tray and serve with remaining sauce. If serving more than 6, double the sauce recipe.

Serve with wild rice casserole.

Barbary French Casserole

3 pounds cubed meat	1 cup sliced onion
¼ cup flour	2 minced garlic cloves
1½ teaspoons salt	1 teaspoon paprika
½ teaspoon fresh ground pepper	1½ cups vin rose wine
2½ tablespoons cooking oil	½ cup water
	½ cup tomato paste
	1 cup sour cream

Dredge meat cubes in flour, salt, and pepper. Heat oil in heavy skillet. Brown meat. Add onion and garlic and cook until onion is limp. Transfer to casserole.

Blend the paprika, wine, water, and tomato paste in drippings in skillet. Pour over meat in casserole. Cover and cook over low heat or bake in 300° oven 1½ hours or until fork tender. Just before serving stir in the sour cream. Serve with rice or noodles. Serves 6-8.

Barbary Filets

These are absolutely delicious and even more tender than beef filets. Wrap in bacon. Brush with melted butter. Place over hot coals on barbecue grill. Broil 10-15 minutes per side or longer depending on thickness of the steaks. Add salt and pepper and brush with more butter as they cook. Allow 1-2 filets per person.

Barbary Steak A La Lorraine

This is a great recipe to serve guests. It is fast, easy, and fun.

6 steaks (½-¾ inches thick)	¼ cup chopped parsley or parsley flakes
¼ cup cooking oil	1 tablespoon lemon juice
1 garlic clove	1 teaspoon Worcester-
¼ cup butter	shire sauce
½ teaspoon salt	¼ teaspoon fresh ground
1 teaspoon Dijon mustard	pepper

Quarter garlic clove. Let stand in oil 30 minutes. Discard garlic. Brush both sides of steaks with oil mixture. Stir butter, mustard, and salt in heated electric skillet. Stir in parsley and cook until butter bubbles. Place steaks in skillet. Turn to coat both sides. Cook steaks 8-10 minutes on each side or to desired doneness. Remove steaks. Stir lemon juice, Worcestershire sauce, and pepper into drippings. Heat and pour over steaks. Serves 6.

Braised Barbary Steak

Use the less tender steak cuts for this recipe. Season steaks with unseasoned meat tenderizer, salt, and pepper. Coat steaks with flour. Brown in 1½ tablespoons cooking oil. Add 1 can (10½ oz.) consommé. Cover and cook slowly until fork tender, usually ¾ to 1½ hours, depending on thickness of meat. Add water if needed during cooking. Thicken pan juices for gravy. Allow 1 large or 2 small steaks per person.

Barbary Kebabs

2-3 pounds boneless steaks cut into 1½ inch cubes	6-8 slices bacon
	½ pound fresh mushrooms
Instant meat tenderizer	1 can (13¼ oz.) pineapple chunks
½ cup bottled French dressing	½ teaspoon salt
1 garlic clove	¼ teaspoon pepper

Sprinkle cubes of meat with meat tenderizer. Chop garlic clove and add to the French dressing. Let meat stand in dressing for several hours, covered, in the refrigerator. Remove meat from dressing.

Carefully wash mushrooms and remove stems. The stems may be stored in the refrigerator for use in another recipe. Thread bacon, meat cubes, mushrooms, and pineapple chunks on 6 skewers. Season with salt and pepper. Broil over hot coals, basting with dressing mix, and turning frequently until done. If desired wrap kebabs in foil, covering with remaining French dressing and sealing. Bake in 350° oven 20-30 minutes. Serves 6.

Barbary Roast

3-4 pound roast	½ teaspoon fresh ground pepper
2 garlic cloves	
3-4 thin strips salt pork	

Cut gashes in meat. Insert pieces of garlic in cuts. Pepper roast. Cover with salt pork. Wrap in aluminum foil. Roast in 325° oven 2½-3 hours. Test for doneness. Remove roast from foil to heated platter. Pour juices from foil into a saucepan. Add 1 cup water and 1 beef bouillon cube. Heat until cube is melted. Thicken and season gravy. Serves 6-8.

Barbary Sheep Burger

Since the fat and tallow have been removed, sheep burger is very lean. Mix beef hamburger with the sheep burger (about 2 to 1). This can be used in any of the ground meat recipes.

Barbary Sheep Liver

Soak the liver in salt water in case there is a tendency for a strong taste. Roll thin slices of liver in seasoned corn meal, and fry in butter or bacon grease.

Bear

If the bear is young and tender it may be cooked like beef. The meat resembles a beef round, although it is a darker red and more coarse. Make sure bear meat is always cooked well done. Older bear meat may be stewed, braised, or cooked in a pressure cooker. Trim every bit of fat away because any wild animal cooked in its own fat will take on a gamey taste. Use butter, bacon, or salt pork for larding. Tougher cuts or stringy meat may be ground for dog food, although, again, be sure it is well cooked. Tender cuts, such as the loin, may be corned, or cured and smoked.

Braised Bear Steak

4-6 steaks	4 tablespoons fat
¼ cup flour	1½ cups bouillon
1 teaspoon salt	1 cup red wine
¼ teaspoon pepper	2 cups tomato paste
1 cup sliced onion	

Pound flour and seasonings into steak with edge of plate or meat pounder. Brown onion in fat and remove. Brown meat well on both sides. Return onion. Add part of the broth and wine, and bring to boil. Cook 5 minutes.

Turn the steak. Reduce heat, cover the pan, and simmer 1½ hours adding more liquid when necessary. When steak is tender, remove to hot platter. Add the tomato paste, the rest of the wine, and bouillon. Cook to a smooth sauce. Pour over the steak. Serves 4-6.

Cottage Fried Bear Steak

Use tender steak for this. Cut 4-6 steaks ¼ inch thick. Season with salt, pepper, and garlic salt. Dredge in flour. Brown in hot fat. Reduce heat and simmer, covered, 30-40 minutes until well done. Serves 4.

Bear Roast

4-5 pound round or rump roast	1 garlic clove
1 teaspoon salt	½ cup butter
¼ teaspoon pepper	Meat tenderizer (unseasoned)

Sprinkle bear roast with tenderizer. Trim all fat from roast. Make gashes in the meat and insert pieces of garlic. Season with salt and pepper. Cover with butter. Wrap the roast loosely in aluminum foil. Roast in 325° oven 3-4 hours. Test for doneness. Serves 6-8.

Bear Pot Roast

2 pound boneless pot roast	Gravy:
1 tablespoon fat	3 tablespoons flour
½ teaspoon salt	1 cup tomato juice
¼ teaspoon pepper	1 cup water
¼ cup flour	½ teaspoon celery salt
1 sliced onion	1 teaspoon Worcestershire sauce
¼ cup red wine	
¼ cup water	

Melt the fat in a heavy skillet or dutch oven. Dredge the bear steak in seasoned flour. Brown on both sides in the hot fat. Add the onion, wine, and water. Cover and simmer 3 hours or more adding more water if necessary. Remove meat to a hot platter. Stir flour into the drippings. Slowly add tomato juice and water. Cook over low heat, stirring constantly until gravy is thickened. Add the celery salt and Worcestershire sauce. Add more salt and pepper if necessary. Serve in gravy boat with meat. Serves 4.

Bear Steak with Port

1½ pounds round steak	¼ teaspoon marjoram
2 tablespoons butter	¼ cup port wine
1 can (2 oz.) sliced	½ cup water
mushrooms	1 tablespoon honey
½ teaspoon salt	1 tablespoon cornstarch
¼ teaspoon pepper	or flour
½ teaspoon grated	2 tablespoons water
lemon rind	

Cut bear steak into thin strips. Sauté slowly in butter until brown turning often. Add mushrooms, salt, pepper, lemon rind, marjoram, honey, and wine. Cover and simmer 1 hour or more. Remove cover. Blend cornstarch or flour with the 2 tablespoons water. Slowly stir into meat mixture. Cook over low heat until thickened. Serve with rice or noodles. Serves 4.

Buffalo

Buffalo was the most prominent food for the American Indian, traders, travelers, and settlers, and was said to be the finest meat on the continent. It is very rich and easily digestable. The flesh is juicy, flavorful, and much like good beef. The tongue is a great delicacy as is the hump.

Only a few states still permit buffalo hunting. However, the animals are on the increase and closely regulated hunting is becoming more popular. You can also purchase a buffalo, either live or butchered, from surplus animals on refuges from the U.S. Fish and Wildlife Service.

Filet of Bison

Trim all fat from one whole filet of bison. Prepare a hot marinade and pour over filet. Cover and keep in the refrigerator 2-3 days. Remove from marinade. Place slices of salt pork on filet. Tie with a cord to hold its shape.

In large roasting pan brown filet in ½ cup butter. Lower heat and add 2 cans (10½ oz. each) beef bouillon, 2 sliced onions, ½ teaspoon freshly ground pepper, a pinch of tarragon, marjoram, and mace. Place in 300° oven and roast 4-5 hours or until done. Baste occasionally with marinade. Slice and serve with thickened gravy made from pan juices. Depending on size of loin, this will serve from 15-20 people.

Stew
and
Ground Meat

Stew

Stew is a universal dish and almost any wild game is delicious stewed. After steaks, roasts, and ribs are cut, the large portions of more tender meat may be cut in 1 or 1½ inch cubes. These various stew meat cuts are derived from:

Shoulder meat—makes excellent lean and tender stew meat.

Rump or round—use the less tender portions of the round and cut across the grain. This is lean and fine flavored.

Neck—this is less tender and needs longer cooking.

Shank or foreleg—this is coarse meat with much gristle, and a tenderizer should be used on it.

Brisket, plate, or flank—this is hard to debone, but is lean and flavorful.

Stew meat may be coated in flour and browned in fat for a brown stew or cooked plain for a light stew. All stews should be cooked slowly or pressured by a moist cooking method. They may be cooked on top of the stove or in the oven, using a dutch oven or a casserole with a tight lid.

Allow 1 pound of stew meat for 4 servings. Stew is often better after sitting, and extra portions may be frozen.

Bourguignon

2 pounds tender stew
   meat cut in 1 inch
   cubes
4 slices bacon
1 can (10½ oz.) beef
   broth (bouillon)
1¼ cups water

2 minced garlic cloves
1 bay leaf
8-10 small, whole,
   white onions
5 carrots cut in 2 inch
   pieces
1 can (4 oz.) sliced

mushrooms	1 cup sherry
2 tablespoons flour	Salt and pepper to taste

Cook bacon until lightly crisped. Remove. Cut into small pieces. Brown meat in bacon drippings. Drain. Sprinkle with salt and pepper. Add bacon, soup, 1 cup of the water, ½ cup wine, garlic, and bay leaf. Cover and simmer 1 hour, stirring occasionally. Add onions and carrots. Simmer 1 more hour. Remove bay leaf. Blend flour with the remaining ¼ cup water. Push meat to one side and stir flour mixture into sauce. Cook slowly and blend in other ½ cup of wine. Serve with rice or noodles. Serves 4.

Bourbon Ragout

2 pounds stew meat cut in cubes	1 teaspoon salt
2 tablespoons cooking oil	½ teaspoon pepper
1 diced onion	2 tablespoons brown bead sauce or gravy seasoning
1 diced carrot	
1 can (10½ oz.) beef consommé	⅓ cup bourbon
2 tablespoons tomato purée	2 tablespoons chopped parsley

Brown meat in cooking oil. Place in casserole. Brown the onion and carrot in drippings. Place on meat. Add the consommé, tomato purée, salt, and pepper. Cover and bake in 350° oven for 1½ hours. Add the brown bead sauce and bourbon. Sprinkle with parsley and serve with brown rice or noodles. Serves 4.

Brandy-Wise Stew

2 pounds very tender stew meat cut in thin strips	1 can (10½ oz.) beef broth
2 tablespoons butter	1 can (10¾ oz.) tomato soup
½ pound sliced mushrooms	1 teaspoon salt
	½ teaspoon pepper

1 teaspoon paprika   ¼ cup evaporated milk
1 egg   ¼ cup brandy

Brown meat in butter. Pour in 2 tablespoons of the brandy. Add the mushrooms and simmer 5 minutes. Add broth and soup. Season with salt, pepper, and paprika. Simmer 5 minutes more. Mix egg with milk and stir in with remaining brandy. Serves 4.

Cantonese Skillet

1½ pounds very tender
   stew meat
½ cup flour
2 tablespoons shortening
3 tablespoons brown
   sugar
1 teaspoon salt
1 tablespoon soy sauce
1 teaspoon Worcester-
   shire sauce

½ cup beef bouillon
   (1 bouillon cube dis-
   solved in 1 cup boil-
   ing water)
¼ cup cider
1 can (13¼ oz.) pine-
   apple tidbits
1 green pepper cut
   in thin rounds
1 onion sliced thin

Cut stew meat in thin strips. Coat with ¼ cup of the flour. Brown in shortening in skillet. Cover and cook 10 minutes. Mix sugar, remaining flour, salt, cider, soy sauce, and Worcestershire sauce to smooth paste. Pour over meat. Add bouillon, pineapple, and juice. Simmer 10 minutes. Add green pepper and onion. Cook 5 minutes more. Serve with Chinese noodles. Serves 4.

Chili, Tureen Hot

2 pounds stew meat
Juice of 1 lemon
2 tablespoons bacon
   drippings or shortening
1 large, chopped onion
1 minced garlic clove
1 teaspoon cumin seed
½ teaspoon oregano
2 tablespoons chili

   powder
1 can (4 oz.) chopped
   green chili
1 can (29 oz.) tomatoes
1 teaspoon salt
¼ teaspoon pepper
1 tablespoon sugar
1 cup water or more

Sprinkle meat with lemon juice. Brown the meat

in drippings or shortening. Remove. Sauté onion and garlic until limp. Drain. Return meat and add cumin seed, oregano, chili powder, green chili, tomatoes, salt, pepper, and sugar. Simmer 1½ hours stirring occasionally and adding water as needed. Serve in heated tureen or chafing dish. Accompany with seasoned pinto beans or posole. Serves 6.

Dark Brown Stew

2 pounds stew meat	5 peeled, quartered
1½ teaspoons salt	potatoes
½ teaspoon pepper	4 peeled, quartered
2 tablespoons shortening	onions
¼ cup flour	4 carrots cut in thirds
1½ cups strong coffee	1 diced garlic clove

Roll meat in seasoned flour. Brown in shortening. Add 1 cup coffee. Put in pressure cooker and cook 20-30 minutes. Add vegetables and remaining coffee and cook 6 minutes more. Thicken gravy with remaining flour.

If you do not wish to use a pressure cooker, simmer the meat 1½ hours. Add vegetables and simmer 30-40 minutes more adding more coffee as needed. Serves 6.

Cantonese Skillet Goulash

2 pounds stew meat	1 teaspoon salt
3 tablespoons shortening	½ teaspoon pepper
5 peeled, diced potatoes	2 teaspoons caraway seed
4 peeled, diced onions	1 can (10½ oz.) beef
1 diced garlic clove	broth

Sauté onion and garlic in shortening until transparent. Drain. Add meat, seasonings, and broth. Pressure cook 30 minutes. Add potatoes and caraway seed and cook 4 minutes more.

Or simmer meat, onion, garlic, salt, and pepper 1½ hours. Add potatoes and caraway seed and simmer 30 minutes adding water as needed. Serves 4-6.

Goulash with Sauerkraut

2 pounds stew meat	1 teaspoon salt
3 tablespoons shortening	¼ teaspoon pepper
3 sliced onions	1 teaspoon celery seed
1 diced garlic clove	1 can (16 oz.) sauerkraut
1½ teaspoons paprika	¼ cup cooked rice
1 cup water	½ pint sour cream

Brown onion and garlic in fat. Drain. Add meat. Cover with water. Pressure cook 30 minutes or simmer 1½ hours. Add paprika, salt, pepper, celery seed, and sauerkraut. Bring to boil. Reduce heat, and add rice. Cover and simmer 5 minutes. Fold in sour cream. Serves 6.

Herbed Casserole

2 pounds tender stew meat	¼ teaspoon marjoram
3 slices bacon	¼ teaspoon rosemary
2 diced onions	¼ teaspoon thyme
½ cup red wine	1 bay leaf
1 peeled, chopped tomato	1 can (2 oz.) mushrooms
3 tablespoons flour	1 can (10½ . oz.) beef broth
1 teaspoon salt	2 tablespoons minced parsley
¼ teaspoon pepper	

Fry bacon until crisp. Remove and crumble. Brown meat in drippings. Remove and place in casserole. Sauté onion until limp. Place over meat. Mix flour with drippings and stir until smooth. Add chopped tomato and broth. Cook 3 minutes. Add bacon. Pour over meat. Add wine, salt, pepper, and herbs. Bake in 350° oven 1½ hours adding more wine if needed. Serves 4.

Hungarian Goulash

2 pounds stew meat	2 minced garlic cloves
4 sliced onions	½ teaspoon marjoram
2 tablespoons shortening	4 tablespoons paprika
1 bay leaf	2 cans (10½ oz. each)

chicken consommé	1 teaspoon salt
2 peeled, chopped	¼ teaspoon pepper
tomatoes	

Cook onion and garlic in shortening until limp. Remove. Brown meat in drippings. Mix in spices, tomatoes, and consommé. Pressure cook 30 minutes or simmer 1½-2 hours. Serve with dumplings or noodles. Serves 4-6.

Indian Curry

2 pounds tender	Pinch of saffron
stew meat	¼ teaspoon chili powder
2 chopped onions	2 teaspoons curry powder
1 minced garlic clove	1½ tablespoons soy
1 tablespoon lemon juice	sauce
1 teaspoon salt	2 tablespoons cooking oil
1 teaspoon powdered	1 can (10½ oz.) beef
ginger or 1 tablespoon	bouillon
chopped, fresh ginger	

Brown onion and garlic in oil. Remove. Brown meat in drippings. Return onion and garlic. Sprinkle with lemon juice. Add seasonings, soy sauce, and bouillon. Cover and simmer 40 minutes. Serve with rice and condiments, such as chutney, India relish, chopped, fresh coconut, candied ginger, chopped peanuts, grated, hard-boiled egg, chopped apple and raisins, orange sections, pineapple cubes, crumbled bacon and small green onions. Serves 4.

Irish Stew

2 pounds stew meat	3 diced turnips
¼ cup flour	4 sliced stalks celery
1 teaspoon salt	2 large, diced onions
¼ teaspoon pepper	4 cubed potatoes
¼ teaspoon marjoram	2 tablespoons minced
¼ teaspoon thyme	parsley
1 bay leaf	1 can (10½ oz.) beef
3 tablespoons shortening	bouillon
5 diced carrots	

Mix flour with salt, pepper, marjoram, and thyme. Coat meat with seasoned flour. Brown in shortening. Cover with bouillon and bay leaf. Pressure cook 30 minutes or simmer 2 hours. Remove bay leaf and add vegetables. Add water if needed. Pressure 6 minutes or simmer 30 minutes more. Thicken liquid with flour paste or cook dumplings when starting the vegetables by placing on top and cooking the last 20 minutes. Serves 6.

Juniper Stew

2 pounds stew meat	1 teaspoon salt
2 diced onions	½ cup red wine
1 minced garlic clove	1 can (10½ oz.) golden
3 slices bacon	mushroom soup
1 bay leaf	4 quartered carrots
6 juniper berries	3-4 peeled, quartered
6 whole peppercorns	potatoes

Cook bacon until almost crisp. Remove and cut in small pieces. Add onion and garlic and sauté until transparent. Remove. Brown meat in drippings. Place meat, bacon, onion, and garlic in pressure cooker. Add juniper berries, bay leaf, peppercorns, and salt. Cover with ¼ cup wine and half can mushroom soup. Pressure 20 minutes or cover and simmer 1½ hours adding water as needed. Add carrots and potatoes and rest of the wine and soup. Pressure 6 minutes or simmer 30 minutes until vegetables are done. Remove bay leaf, berries, and peppercorns. Serve with dumplings or biscuits. Serves 6.

Onion Goulash

1½ pounds stew meat	½ teaspoon pepper
2 large, chopped onions	2 tablespoons paprika
2 tablespoons shortening	1 can (10½ oz.) beef
1 tablespoon flour	bouillon
1 teaspoon salt	

Sauté onion in shortening. Remove. Mix flour, salt, pepper, and paprika. Roll meat in mixture. Brown meat in drippings. Add bouillon. Cover and simmer 1 hour adding water if needed. Serves 4.

Pepper Ragout

2 pounds stew meat	¼ teaspoon pepper
¼ pound spicy sausage	2 large, diced green
2 diced onions	peppers
2 tablespoons paprika	1 can (10¾ oz.) tomato
1 teaspoon salt	soup

Brown sausage. Drain. Cook onion until limp. Remove. Fry meat in drippings. Season with salt, pepper, and paprika. Return onion and broken up sausage to pan. Cover with tomato soup and simmer 1 hour adding water as needed. Add green pepper and continue cooking 20 minutes. Serves 4.

Rancher's Stew

2 pounds stew meat	1 tablespoon Worcester-
2 tablespoons shortening	shire sauce
1 chopped onion	1 tablespoon dry mustard
3 tablespoons flour	Juice of ½ lemon
1 teaspoon salt	½ teaspoon parsley
¼ teaspoon pepper	1 can (10½ oz.) beef
½ teaspoon savory	bouillon
¼ teaspoon oregano	

Sauté onion in shortening. Dust meat with flour. Brown in drippings. Stir in bouillon. Add salt, pepper, savory, and oregano. Simmer 1½ hours. Add Worcestershire sauce, mustard, and lemon juice. Cook 10 minutes more. Add parsley and serve. Serves 4.

Savory Viand

2 pounds stew meat	2 cups diced potatoes
2 tablespoons shortening	1 cup diced onion
3 tablespoons flour	1 bay leaf
1 teaspoon salt	2 tablespoons minced
1 cup diced carrots	parsley
1 cup diced celery	½ teaspoon thyme

Stir salt and pepper into flour. Dredge meat in flour. Brown slowly in hot shortening in dutch oven or heavy skillet. Cover with water and simmer, covered, 1½ hours. Add the vegetables, bay leaf, parsley, thyme, and beef gravy. Simmer 30 minutes more adding water if necessary. Serves 6.

Spanish Stew

2 pounds stew meat	½ teaspoon pepper
1 large, sliced onion	1 teaspoon paprika
2 tablespoons shortening	1 tablespoon parsley
1 minced garlic clove	1 tablespoon chervil
1 can (12 oz.) tomato	12 cubed, small, new
paste	potatoes or 4 large
1 cup red wine	potatoes
1 teaspoon salt	3 Polish or hot sausages

Sauté onion and garlic in shortening. Remove. Brown meat in drippings. Place meat in casserole. Add onion and garlic. Add tomato paste, wine, salt, pepper, and herbs. Simmer 1 hour. Add the potatoes and sliced sausage. Simmer 30 minutes more adding more water if necessary. Serves 6.

Stroganoff #1

1 pound very tender	mix
stew meat	2 tablespoons flour
2 tablespoons butter	1 cup milk
1 can (6 oz.) sliced	1 cup water
mushrooms (or sautéed	½ cup sour cream
½ pound fresh)	Boiled noodles
1 package onion soup	

Cut stew meat in thin pieces. Brown in butter. Add mushrooms and soup mix. Stir in flour, milk, and water. Cover and simmer 45 minutes stirring occasionally. Blend in sour cream and heat. Serve over noodles. Serves 4-6.

Stroganoff #2

1 pound very tender
  stew meat
2 tablespoons butter
½ cup chopped onions
1 can (4 oz.) button
  mushrooms
¼ teaspoon dry mustard

1 teaspoon salt
¼ teaspoon pepper
1 package (8 oz.)
  cream cheese
⅔ cup milk
Cooked butter-parsleyed
  noodles

Cut stew meat in thin strips. Brown meat and onions in butter. Add mushrooms, dry mustard, salt, and pepper. Simmer 45 minutes adding small amount of water as needed. Add cream cheese and milk. Stir until cheese melts. Serve over hot butter-parsleyed noodles. Serves 4-6.

Stroganoff #3

2 pounds very tender
  stew meat
⅓ cup flour
1 teaspoon salt
¼ teaspoon pepper
1 cup chopped onion
1 can (8 oz.) sliced

  mushrooms
1 can (10½ oz.) beef
  gravy
½ cup sherry wine
1 pint sour cream
3 tablespoons butter

Cut meat into thin strips. Sprinkle with flour, salt, and pepper. Brown with onions in butter. Add mushrooms, beef gravy, and wine. Cover and simmer about 45 minutes or until tender. Stir in sour cream and serve over noodles or rice. Serves 6-8.

Western Stew

2 pounds stew meat
3 tablespoons lemon
  juice
2 tablespoons shortening
1 teaspoon salt
¼ teaspoon pepper

2 tablespoons chili
  powder
2 bouillon cubes
2 cups boiling water
1 cup pitted and sliced
  ripe olives

Sprinkle meat with lemon juice. Let stand 2-3

hours. Mix flour with salt, pepper, and chili powder. Roll meat in mixture. Brown in shortening. Add bouillon cubes and cover with boiling water. Cover and simmer 2 hours. Add olives. Heat and stir. Serve with Spanish rice. Serves 6-8.

Ground Meat

Wild game meat will greatly enhance the flavor of beef hamburger when mixed ½ of each depending on the leanness. For delicious meat loaves add ⅓ ground veal, ⅓ ground beef, and ⅓ ground pork, or buy the meat loaf mixture and mix with ⅓ ground wild meat.

All-in-one Casserole

1 pound ground meat	1 can (16 oz.) tomatoes
2 cups sliced, raw potatoes	2 teaspoons salt
2 cups diced celery	½ teaspoon pepper
1 cup sliced onion	1 can (10½ oz.) beef consommé
1 cup sliced green pepper	

Place in layers in greased casserole. Cover with consommé and bake in 350° oven 1½ hours. Serves 4.

Applesauce Meatballs

1 pound ground meat	1 teaspoon salt
½ cup soft bread crumbs	¼ teaspoon pepper
1 egg	½ cup unsweetened applesauce
2 tablespoons minced onion	

The addition of applesauce makes these meatballs very tender and moist.

Shape into 2 inch balls. Brown in hot fat. Place in baking dish. Pour over a mixture of ½ cup catsup and ½ cup water. Cover and bake in 350° oven 45 minutes. Serves 4.

Burgundy Meatballs

1½ pounds ground meat
1 egg
½ cup soft bread crumbs
¼ cup milk
1½ teaspoons salt
½ teaspoon garlic salt
3 tablespoons butter
6-8 chopped, small, white onions

1 can (4 oz.) button mushrooms (or ½ pound fresh)
1 teaspoon sugar
⅓ cup flour
1 can (10½ oz.) beef bouillon
1 cup Burgundy wine
1 bay leaf

Mix meat, egg, bread crumbs, milk, 1 teaspoon of salt, and garlic salt. Shape into 12 balls. Brown meatballs in butter. Add onions and mushrooms and sprinkle with sugar. Cook until onions are clear. Remove to baking pan. Blend flour and ½ teaspoon salt into drippings. Stir in bouillon until smooth. Pour over meatballs. Add wine and bay leaf. Simmer 40-45 minutes. Remove bay leaf. Put in heated serving dish. Sprinkle with chopped parsley. Serves 6.

Baked Burger Rice

1 pound ground meat
1 cup rice
1 chopped onion
1 teaspoon salt
½ teaspoon pepper

1 teaspoon paprika
½ cup sliced olives
2 cups tomato juice
1½ cups boiling water
½ cup grated cheese

Brown meat and add rice and onion. Cook until light brown. Add tomato juice, olives, seasonings, and boiling water. Place in casserole. Cover and bake in 300° oven 1 hour. Uncover, sprinkle with cheese and bake 10 minutes longer. Serves 4-6.

Burger-Chili Patties

1 pound ground meat
1 teaspoon salt
¼ teaspoon pepper
1 egg

2 tablespoons cooking oil
2 tablespoons chopped, onion
2 tablespoons chopped,

<table>
<tr><td>green chili</td><td>1 tablespoon chili</td></tr>
<tr><td>1 can (12 oz.) tomatoes</td><td>powder</td></tr>
<tr><td>1 can (8¾ oz.) corn</td><td></td></tr>
</table>

Combine meat, salt, pepper, and egg. Shape into patties and place in baking dish. Cook onions in oil until limp. Place onions over patties. Add tomatoes, corn, green chili, and chili powder. Bake in 325° oven 35 minutes. Serves 4.

Burritos

1 pound ground meat	2 cans (4 oz. each) green
2 tablespoons minced	chili or 4 roasted,
onion	peeled, and diced fresh
1 can (8 oz.) tomato	1 finely diced, medium,
sauce	cooked potato
1 package flour tortillas	

Brown meat slowly. Add onion, green chili, and potato. Cover and simmer until onion is limp. Add tomato sauce. Simmer 5 minutes more. Place a tablespoon of filling on a flour tortilla and roll. Heat with red or green chili sauce. Serves 4.

Barbecued Burgers

2 pounds ground meat	2 tablespoons prepared
2 tablespoons chopped	mustard
green pepper	1 teaspoon salt
½ cup chopped onion	½ teaspoon pepper
½ cup catsup	2 tablespoons sugar
2 tablespoons chili sauce	1 tablespoon vinegar

Slowly fry onions and green pepper in fat until limp. Remove. Brown meat in drippings. Add other ingredients and simmer 5 minutes. Serve on buns. Serves 6.

Calico Pie

1 pound ground meat	flavored bits
½ cup bread crumbs	1 teaspoon salt
2 tablespoons bacon	½ teaspoon pepper

1 egg
1 can (15 oz.) Swiss steak
  sauce
½ cup sherry

1 box (10 oz.) frozen
  mixed vegetables
  (cooked)
Package pie crust mix

Mix meat, bread crumbs, ¼ cup sauce, bacon bits, salt, and pepper. Shape into 1 inch balls. Brown slowly in fat. Stir rest of sauce and wine into pan. Heat to simmer. Add vegetables and remove from heat. Prepare pie crust dough. Roll out half to fit bottom of 9 inch pie plate. Spoon meat mixture into crust. Roll out rest of pastry and fit over top. Trim and flute. Cut several slits in top. Bake in 400° oven 45 minutes. Serve in wedges. Serves 6.

Chili Con Carne

1 pound ground meat
1 chopped onion
1 chopped garlic clove
1 teaspoon salt
½ teaspoon oregano

½ teaspoon cumin seed
4-5 tablespoons chili
  powder
1 can (29-oz.) tomatoes
½ cup red wine or water

Brown onion and garlic in fat. Remove. Brown meat slowly and drain all grease. Return all to pan. Add tomatoes, chili powder, spices, and wine. Simmer 1½-2 hours. Serve over hot pinto beans, or serve beans on the side. Serves 6.

Chili Picante

If you prefer chili less hot, use mild chilis and mild sauce.

1 pound ground meat
1 large, diced onion
1 diced garlic clove
1 teaspoon salt
½ teaspoon pepper
1 can (4 oz.) diced chilis

(hot)
1 can (10 oz.) enchilada
  sauce (hot)
1 can (29 oz.) tomatoes
1 can (15 oz.) pinto beans
  (with chili sauce)

Sauté onion and garlic 5 minutes. Remove. Brown meat slowly separating with fork. Drain all fat. Add chilis, salt, pepper, and sauce. Simmer 30 minutes. Add tomatoes slightly broken up. Simmer 10 minutes. Add beans and heat. Serves 6-8.

Chili Verdes

1 pound ground meat	1 can (8 oz.) green chili
1 diced onion	sauce
1 diced garlic clove	1 can (4 oz.) diced green
1 teaspoon salt	chilis
¼ teaspoon oregano	1 can (8 oz.) tomato
½ teaspoon pepper	sauce

Brown onion and garlic. Remove. Brown meat; drain off all fat. Return onion and garlic. Add oregano, chili sauce, green chilis, and tomato sauce. Simmer 30 minutes. Serves 4-6.

Chili Meat Loaf

1½ pounds ground meat	2 eggs
½ cup chopped onion	1 can (4 oz.) diced green
¼ cup chopped green	chili (drained)
pepper	Bouillon cube dissolved
1 diced garlic clove	in ½ cup boiling water
1 teaspoon salt	3 tablespoons butter
¼ teaspoon pepper	3 tablespoons bread
2 tablespoons chili	crumbs
powder	

Mix meat with onions, green pepper, garlic, and green chilis. Season with salt, pepper, and chili powder. Beat the eggs lightly with broth. Work into meat mixture. Put in greased baking dish (loaf pan). Dot with butter and bread crumbs. Bake in 350° oven 1 hour 15 minutes. Serve with chili sauce. Serves 6.

Cordon Bleu Patties

2 pounds ground meat	Thin-sliced, boiled ham
1 package green-onion	2 eggs
dip mix	1 cup fine cracker crumbs
Sliced Swiss cheese	2 tablespoons cooking oil

Mix meat and dip mix until well blended. Divide into 12 equal parts. On waxed paper pat out each to a rectangle 3x4 inches. Top 6 pieces with a piece of cheese, then a piece of ham. Cover with another meat piece. Press the edges together to seal.

Beat eggs slightly in shallow pan. Dip each patty into egg, then in cracker crumbs. Saute slowly in hot cooking oil, allowing 8 minutes per side, or until cooked thoroughly. Serves 6.

Crêpes Continental

Pancake mix	1½ pounds ground meat
5 tablespoons butter	1 cup grated Parmesan
3 tablespoons flour	cheese
1 teaspoon salt	½ cup chopped onion
¼ teaspoon pepper	1 can (4 oz.) sliced
2½ cups milk	mushrooms

Make crêpes and bake according to mix recipe. Melt butter. Blend in flour, ½ teaspoon salt, and half the pepper. Add milk and cook until sauce thickens. Remove from heat. Stir in ¾ cup of the cheese.

Sauté onion until soft. Remove. Brown meat breaking apart with fork. Stir in cheese sauce, mushrooms, rest of salt, and pepper. Spoon 2 tablespoons on each crepe. Roll up. Place on baking sheet. Cover with rest of sauce. Bake in 375° oven 20 minutes. Serves 6-8.

Empanadas (Meat Turnovers)

½ pound ground meat	1 can (2¼ oz.) deviled
1 package pie crust mix	ham
¼ cup chopped onion	¼ cup chopped, ripe
1 teaspoon chili powder	olives
1 can (15½ oz.) refried	¼ cup chopped pimiento
beans	1 egg
1 teaspoon salt	2 tablespoons milk

Sauté onion until soft. Remove. Brown meat and return onion. Add chili powder, beans, and salt. Simmer a few minutes. Stir in ham, olives, and pimiento.

Prepare pie crust mix and divide into thirds. Roll out ⅛ inch thick. Cut into 4 inch rounds. Place 1 table-spoon of the filling on one half of each round and fold other half over filling. Press edges together to seal. Cut several slits in top. Place 1 inch apart on cookie sheet. Beat egg slightly and mix with milk. Brush on turnovers. Bake in 400° oven 20 minutes. Serves 4-6.

Enchiladas

2 pounds ground meat	sauce
2 tablespoons red chili powder	2 cans (8 oz. each) enchilada sauce
2 diced onions	2 cans (4 oz. each) diced green chilis
1 diced garlic clove	
2½ cups shredded Cheddar cheese	1 can (5¾ oz.) pitted ripe olives
1 can (8 oz.) tomato	Tortillas

Sauté onions and garlic and remove from pan. Brown meat separating with fork. Add chili powder, salt, and pepper. Dip tortillas in enchilada sauce. Add meat to center of tortilla. Top with grated cheese, chopped green chili, and 3-4 ripe olives. Roll up and place in baking pan. Top all with more sauce, grated cheese, and olives. Bake in 350° oven 30-40 minutes. Serves 6.

Lasagne

1 pound ground meat	glutamate
2 tablespoons cooking oil	1 can (29 oz.) tomatoes
½ cup diced onion	1 can (6 oz.) tomato paste
2 mashed garlic cloves	1 cup Parmesan cheese
1 teaspoon salt	1 pound Mozarella cheese
½ teaspoon pepper	
½ teaspoon oregano	1 pound Ricotta cheese
3 bay leaves	1 pound lasagne noodles
1 teaspoon monosodium	

Sauté onions and garlic in oil until transparent. Remove. Brown meat in same skillet and drain all fat. Add the onions and garlic, salt, pepper, oregano, bay leaves, monosodium glutamate, tomatoes, and tomato paste. Add ¼ cup of the Parmesan cheese. Cover and simmer 30 minutes.

Meanwhile cook lasagne noodles in boiling, salted water until white and tender. Drain and rise with cold water. In large baking dish arrange ⅓ of the meat mixture. Cover with 1 layer of noodles, layer of Mozarella, layer of Ricotta, and 2 tablespoons Parmesan. Repeat, ending with sauce and Parmesan. Bake in 350° oven 30 minutes. Serves 4-6.

Macaroni Bake

1½ pounds ground meat	broth
½ pound elbow	1 can (10¾ oz.) tomato
macaroni	soup
2 tablespoons butter	1 teaspoon salt
1 diced onion	¼ teaspoon pepper
1 can (29 oz.) tomatoes	¼ cup grated cheese
1 can (10½ oz.) beef	Bread crumbs

Cook macaroni in boiling salted water. Drain and rinse with cold water.

Brown the meat and onion in butter. Drain all fat. Add tomatoes, beef broth, salt, pepper, and tomato. Season. Put macaroni in greased casserole. Cover with meat mixture. Bake in 350° oven 30 minutes. Remove. Top with cheese and crumbs. Place under broiler until browned. Serves 6.

Meat and Noodle-do

1½ pounds ground meat	¼ teaspoon pepper
1 cup diced onion	1 tablespoon Worcester-
3 cups tomato juice	shire sauce
1 teaspoon celery salt	½ pint sour cream
1 teaspoon salt	1 package wide noodles

Sauté the onion in butter until transparent. Add the meat and brown. Put raw noodles over the meat. Add the tomato juice, seasonings, and Worcestershire sauce. Bring to a boil. Reduce heat and simmer 30 minutes. Remove from heat. Stir in sour cream. Serves 6.

German Meatballs

1½ pounds ground meat	1 can (12 oz.) beer
½ cup soft bread crumbs	½ teaspoon thyme
2 cans (10½ oz. each)	½ teaspoon garlic salt
beef broth	¼ teaspoon pepper
½ cup flour	1 tablespoon chopped
2 tablespoons cooking oil	parsley
1 diced onion	

Mix meat with bread crumbs and ½ cup of the broth. Shape in 2 inch balls. Roll meatballs in flour and brown on all sides in cooking oil. Remove from pan. Pour off drippings except for 2 tablespoons. Stir in onion and cook over low heat until soft. Remove. Thicken drippings with 2 tablespoons flour. Stir in rest of broth, beer, and seasonings. Cook over low heat until thickened. Return meatballs and onions to gravy. Simmer 20 minutes adding water if necessary. Place on platter and sprinkle with parsley. Serves 6.

Barbecued Meatballs

2 pounds ground meat	1 teaspoon chili powder
1 teaspoon salt	2 tablespoons Worcester-
¼ teaspoon pepper	shire sauce
3 tablespoons cooking oil	1 tablespoon prepared
½ cup chili sauce	mustard
¼ cup red wine	½ teaspoon Liquid
2 tablespoons brown	Smoke
sugar	

Mix meat, salt, and pepper and form into ½ inch balls. Brown on all sides in cooking oil. Remove and drain. Mix all the other ingredients and simmer 20 minutes. Brush the meatballs with Liquid Smoke and add to the sauce. Simmer 10 more minutes or until sauce is thickened. Serves 6-8.

Meatball Stew Casserole

10-12 peeled, small white
  onions
6-8 carrots halved
  lengthwise
1 package (10 oz.) frozen
  peas
1½ pounds ground meat
1 egg
1 cup bread crumbs
¾ teaspoon marjoram
1½ teaspoons salt
Instant mashed potatoes

½ teaspoon pepper
1 teaspoon Worcester-
  shire sauce
⅔ cup milk
¼ cup cooking oil
1 can (4 oz.) mushrooms
1 can (10½ oz.) cream
  of mushroom soup
¾ teaspoon nutmeg
1 teaspoon monosodium
  glutamate

Cook onions and carrots in boiling, salted water 20 minutes. Top with peas and let steam.

Mix meat with egg, crumbs, marjoram, salt, pepper, Worcestershire sauce, and milk. Drop by teaspoons into hot oil and brown quickly. Remove. Cook mushrooms until tender. Add soup and nutmeg.

Arrange vegetables in greased casserole. Add meatballs and soup. Sprinkle with monosodium glutamate.

Prepare mashed potatoes and swirl around edge. Bake in 350° oven 30 minutes. Serves 6.

Meat Éclat

1 pound ground meat
2 tablespoons cooking oil
2 tablespoons lemon
  juice
3 tablespoons flour
2 cups half-half

1 teaspoon salt
¼ teaspoon pepper
1 can (2 oz.) sliced
  mushrooms
1 tablespoon horseradish

Brown meat in oil separating with fork. Sprinkle with lemon juice and flour. Stir until smooth. Slowly stir in milk. Cook until thickened. Stir in salt, pepper, mushrooms, and horseradish. Serve on toast. Serves 4.

Meat Loaf

1½ pounds ground meat	1 teaspoon monosodium
1 diced onion	glutamate
1 diced garlic clove	1 tablespoon Worcester-
1 egg	shire sauce
1 teaspoon salt	1 cup oatmeal
¼ teaspoon pepper	1 cup tomato juice

Mix all ingredients, shape and place in loaf pan. Bake in 350° oven 1 hour. Serve with mushroom sauce. Serves 6.

Meat Loaf of Finland

1½ pounds ground meat	1 teaspoon salt
1 diced onion	½ teaspoon fennel seeds
2 tablespoons butter	12 dried apricots
1 egg	6 pitted prunes
1 cup soft bread crumbs	1 teaspoon paprika
1 tablespoon chopped	1 can (10½ oz.) chicken
parsley	gravy

Sauté onion in butter until soft. Remove. Mix meat, bread crumbs, egg, parsley, salt, and fennel seeds until blended. Pat meat mixture into thin rectangle 9x15 inches on waxed paper. Place 6 apricots across short end. Top with a prune and then remaining apricots. Roll up tightly. Place seam side down in greased baking pan. Bake in 350° oven 1½ hours. Remove and cover with heated gravy. Serves 6.

Meat Loaf with Cheese

1½ pounds ground meat	1 cup cracker crumbs
¼ pound chopped	1 egg
prosciutto	¾ cup canned milk
1 cup grated Parmesan	1 teaspoon salt
cheese	½ teaspoon pepper
½ cup chopped onion	1 crushed bay leaf
¼ cup chopped green	½ teaspoon Tabasco
pepper	sauce
¼ cup chopped parsley	½ cup chili sauce

Mix all ingredients except Tabasco and chili sauce. Place in greased loaf pan. Bake in 350° oven 1 hour. Mix the Tabasco sauce and chili sauce and spread over loaf. Allow to stand for 10 minutes before slicing. Serves 6.

Meat-Potato Patties

1 pound ground meat	1 teaspoon salt
2 cups mashed potatoes	½ teaspoon pepper
2 eggs	Tomato slices (½ inch thick)
¼ cup diced onion	
¼ cup finely chopped celery	2 tablespoons melted butter
½ cup tomato juice	

Mix meat, potatoes, eggs, onion, celery, tomato juice, and seasonings. Shape into 8 patties. Place in baking dish. Cover each pattie with a tomato slice. Brush with butter. Bake in 350° oven 30 minutes. Serves 4-6.

Meat Puff

1 pound ground meat	8 slices bread
1 teaspoon salt	2 tablespoons butter
¼ teaspoon pepper	3 slightly beaten eggs
2 tablespoons chopped parsley	2 cups milk
½ cup mayonnaise	¼ teaspoon sage
	½ teaspoon salt

Brown meat slowly separating with fork until done. Drain well. Add salt, pepper, parsley, and mayonnaise. Spread half of bread slices with butter, cover with meat mixture, and top with rest of bread. Place in greased baking pan.

Beat eggs and milk, and add salt and sage. Pour over sandwiches and let stand in refrigerator 1 hour. Bake in 350° oven about 40 minutes or until browned and puffed. Serves 4.

Mushroom-Stuffed Meat Loaf

2 pounds ground meat	¼ cup butter

1 pound sliced mush-
  rooms (leave 6 whole)
1 teaspoon lemon juice
1 finely diced onion
2 teaspoons salt
¼ teaspoon pepper
¼ cup milk
4 cups fresh bread

  crumbs
¼ teaspoon pepper
¼ teaspoon thyme
¼ cup chopped parsley
2 eggs
⅓ cup catsup
1½ teaspoons Dijon
  mustard

Sauté sliced mushrooms in butter. Add lemon juice and onion and cook until limp. Add crumbs, 1 teaspoon salt, pepper, thyme, and parsley.

Mix meat, eggs, 1 teaspoon salt, pepper, milk, catsup, and mustard. Pack half of meat mixture into loaf pan. Put all of stuffing on top, then the rest of the meat. Press the 6 whole mushrooms in the top. Bake in 375° oven 1 hour 15 minutes. Brush top with currant jelly. Serves 8.

Noodle Goulash

1 pound ground meat
1 tablespoon shortening
1 diced onion
2 cups diced celery
1 teaspoon salt

¼ teaspoon pepper
Drained hot, boiled
  noodles
1 can (16 oz.) tomatoes
¾ cup shredded cheese

Brown meat in shortening breaking apart as it cooks. Add onion and celery and cook 10 minutes more. Mix in noodles, tomatoes, cheese, salt, and pepper. Simmer 30 minutes. Serves 4.

Onion Burgers

1½ pounds ground meat
½ teaspoon salt
½ teaspoon pepper
1 package onion soup
  mix

2 tablespoons
  horseradish
2 teaspoons dry mustard
Hamburger buns

Combine all ingredients and shape into patties. Place on broiler rack 2 inches from heat. Broil to desired doneness (8-10 minutes per side). Serve on hamburger buns. Serves 4.

Onion Rolls

1½ pounds ground meat
½ cup diced onion
1 cup bread crumbs
⅓ cup barbecue sauce
1 tablespoon horseradish
1 teaspoon Dijon mustard
1 teaspoon salt
¼ teaspoon pepper

2 tablespoons chopped
 parsley
1 egg
½ cup milk
1 package seasoned coat-
 ing for pork chops
1 package onion gravy
 mix

Combine meat, crumbs, barbecue sauce, horse-radish, mustard, salt, egg, and milk. Shape into ten 3 inch rolls. Shake in coating mix. Bake in 350° oven 30 minutes.
Prepare onion gravy mix and pour over rolls. Serves 6.

Oriental Meatballs

2 pounds ground meat
2 teaspoons fresh ginger
 or ½ teaspoon pow-
 dered ginger
1 teaspoon salt
¼ teaspoon pepper
1 minced onion
½ cup chopped green
 pepper
½ teaspoon monosodium

 glutamate
6 tablespoons soy sauce
¼ cup butter
3 tablespoons flour
1 beef bouillon cube
 dissolved in 1 cup
 boiling water
1 can (20 oz.) chunk
 pineapple and juice

Mix the meat, half the ginger, salt, pepper, onion, and green pepper. Add the monosodium glutamate and 4 tablespoons of the soy sauce working in the meat. Shape in 1½ inch balls. Brown slowly in butter. Remove. Drain and put in casserole. Add flour to drippings and mix to a smooth paste. Add broth, rest of the soy sauce, and ginger. Drain the pineapple and add the juice. Cook slowly stirring constantly until smooth and thickened. Pour over the meatballs. Bake in 350° oven 30 minutes. Spoon pineapple chunks in with the meatballs. These are excellent served as canapés. For these, make meatballs smaller. Serves 6.

Paprikash

1½ pounds ground meat	1 chicken bouillon cube
1 tablespoon cooking oil	dissolved in 1 cup
1½ cups sliced onion	boiling water
2 tablespoons paprika	1 package medium
3 tablespoons flour	noodles
1 garlic clove	¾ cup sour cream
1½ teaspoons salt	Parsley

Brown meat in cooking oil. Turn carefully leaving in chunks. Remove. Stir onion, garlic, and paprika into pan. Cook until onion is soft. Return meat to pan and sprinkle flour and salt over top. Stir in chicken broth. Cook and stir until thickened. Cover and simmer 15 minutes.

Cook noodles in boiling, salted water until tender. Drain. Stir 1 cup of the hot meat mixture into the sour cream, then stir back into meat mixture in pan. Heat slowly. Place noodles on heated platter. Spoon meat mixture over and sprinkle with parsley. Serves 6.

Pizza

1 pound ground meat	¼ teaspoon marjoram
1 can dinner rolls	1 tablespoon Parmesan
¼ cup chopped onion	cheese
1 chopped garlic clove	6 thin slices salami
1 can (16 oz.) tomato	½ pound Mozzarella
sauce	cheese
1 teaspoon salt	1 small (2 oz.) can
½ teaspoon pepper	button mushrooms
¼ teaspoon oregano	

Brown meat, onion, and garlic slowly. Drain all fat off. Add tomato sauce, salt, pepper, oregano, marjoram, and Parmesan cheese. Simmer 15 minutes.

Press dinner rolls thinly in greased pizza pan.

Pull up on edge to form lip. Add meat mixture. Place salami and sliced Mozzarella cheese on meat mixture. Drain mushrooms and add. Bake in 400° oven 12-15 minutes or until crust is puffed and brown. Serves 4.

Pimiento Loaf

1½ pounds ground meat	¼ teaspoon pepper
¾ cup dry bread crumbs	⅓ cup Parmesan cheese
1½ cups tomato juice	¼ cup chopped olives
2 tablespoons lemon juice	2 cans (4 oz. each) whole pimientos
1 egg	1 can (10¾ oz.) beef gravy
1 teaspoon salt	
1 tablespoon dried onion flakes	2 tablespoons sherry

Line loaf pan with foil. Leave overhang around pan. Grease well.

Mix meat, crumbs, ½ cup of tomato juice, lemon juice, egg, salt, pepper, onion flakes, cheese, and olives.

Cut each pimiento into thirds twice (making 6 petals). Cover bottom and sides of greased pan with the petals. Press meat mixture carefully on pimientos.

Bake in 350° oven 1 hour. Lift up on foil to loosen from pan. Turn upside down on platter.

Mix gravy and rest of tomato juice and cook down until thickened. Remove from heat and add sherry. Pour over the meat loaf. Serves 6.

Porcupines

1 pound ground meat	sauce
½ cup bread crumbs	½ teaspoon pepper
½ cup chopped onion	1 cup raw rice
½ chopped green pepper	1 can (10¾ oz.) tomato soup
1 teaspoon salt	1 cup boiling water
1 can (8 oz.) tomato	

Mix meat, crumbs, onion, green pepper, tomato

sauce, salt, and pepper. Shape in 2 inch balls. Roll balls in rice. Place in casserole. Cover with tomato soup and water. Bake in 350° oven 1 hour 15 minutes. Add more water if necessary. Serves 4.

Redskin Stew

1½ pounds ground meat	whole-kernel corn
1 tablespoon butter	1 tablespoon Worcester-
1 chopped onion	shire sauce
1 chopped green pepper	Dash of Tabasco sauce
3 peeled, chopped	1 tablespoon sugar
tomatoes	2 teaspoons salt
1 package (10 oz.) frozen	

Cook onion and green pepper in butter until limp. Remove. Add meat and brown. Drain off all fat. Add corn, tomatoes, seasonings, onion, and green pepper. Simmer 25 minutes. Serves 4-6.

Sour Cream Loaf

1½ pounds ground meat	1 teaspoon salt
2 tablespoons diced	½ teaspoon pepper
onion	½ cup sour cream
2 ground carrots	

Combine all ingredients. Shape into loaf. Bake in 350° oven 1 hour. Serve with mushroom or tomato sauce. Serves 6.

Spaghetti Casserole

1 pound ground meat	sauce
1 diced onion	1 can (10¾ oz.) tomato
1 green pepper	soup
cut in rings	2 tablespoons Parmesan
1 teaspoon garlic salt	cheese
½ teaspoon pepper	1 package thin spaghetti
1 tablespoon Worcester-	4 cups boiling water
shire sauce	1 tablespoon salt
1 can (8 oz.) tomato	½ teaspoon cooking oil

Brown meat separating with fork. Remove and drain. Cook onion and green pepper in drippings.

Cook spaghetti in boiling, salted water to which has been added the ½ teaspoon of oil. Drain and rinse with cold water.

Arrange a layer of spaghetti, seasoning, meat mixture, onion and green pepper, tomato sauce, and soup. Continue until all is used ending with the tomato sauce. Add the Parmesan cheese. Cover and bake in 350° oven 30 minutes. Serves 6.

Italian Spaghetti Sauce

½ pound ground meat	1 teaspoon salt
1 can (29 oz.) tomatoes	¼ teaspoon pepper
1 can (6 oz.) tomato paste	Pinch of red pepper
1 finely chopped garlic	1 teaspoon sugar
clove	¼ cup dried mushrooms
1 large, chopped onion	Parmesan cheese

Brown meat and remove. Sauté onion and garlic in drippings. Drain. Place meat, onion, and garlic in heavy saucepan. Add tomatoes, tomato paste, seasonings, and mushrooms. Reduce heat and simmer 1 hour. Serve over hot, drained, buttered spaghetti. Sprinkle with cheese. Serves 4.

Spicy Meatballs

1½ pounds ground meat	1 teaspoon paprika
1 cup soft bread crumbs	1 teaspoon dry mustard
1 chopped onion	2 eggs
1 finely chopped garlic	1 can (6 oz.) tomato paste
clove	1 can (10½ oz.) beef
1½ teaspoons salt	bouillon
¼ teaspoon pepper	Cooking oil
½ teaspoon nutmeg	½ cup sour cream

Mix meat, crumbs, onion, garlic, seasonings, and eggs. Form into 1½ inch balls. Brown in cooking oil. Add tomato paste and bouillon. Simmer about 20 minutes. Stir in sour cream. Serves 4-6.

Springtime Casserole

1 pound ground meat	1 package (10 oz.)
1 cup diced onion	frozen peas
1 diced garlic clove	1 can (4 oz.) diced
2 tablespoons cooking oil	pimientos
½ cup raw rice	2 tablespoons soy sauce
4 cups water	1 teaspoon salt
1 cup diced potatoes	½ teaspoon pepper
1 cup diced carrots	

Brown meat in cooking oil. Remove. Sauté onion and garlic in drippings. Drain.

Put rice and water in casserole. Add meat mixture, carrots, potatoes, peas, and pimiento. Season with soy sauce, salt, and pepper. Bake in 350° oven 40 minutes. Serves 6.

Stuffed Cabbage Rolls

1 pound ground meat	1 bay leaf
12 large cabbage leaves	2 tablespoons cooking oil
1 cup cooked rice	2 tablespoons brown
1 egg	sugar
⅔ cup milk	1 can (10¾ oz.) tomato
½ cup chopped onion	soup
1 teaspoon salt	½ cup water
¼ teaspoon pepper	

Drop cabbage leaves into boiling, salted water and cook about 5 minutes. Drain. Remove thick center vein.

Mix meat, rice, egg, milk, half of chopped onion, salt, and pepper. Place 1 tablespoon on each cabbage leaf. Roll up and fasten with a toothpick.

Melt oil in skillet. Brown cabbage rolls. Sprinkle with sugar. Cover with soup, water, remaining onion, and bay leaf. Cover and simmer 1 hour adding more water if needed. Serves 6.

Stuffed Green Peppers

1 pound ground meat	1 teaspoon salt
6 peppers	¼ teaspoon pepper
1 chopped onion	¼ teaspoon cinnamon
½ cup rice	1 can (10¾ oz.) beef
1 can (29 oz.) tomatoes	gravy

Cut tops from peppers and remove seeds. Brown meat and remove. Sauté onion in drippings. Add rice, tomatoes, salt, pepper, and cinnamon and cook 15 minutes while stirring. Mix in meat. Stuff the peppers with the mixture. Put tops on to hold in stuffing and arrange in baking dish. Add gravy and 1 cup water. Bake in 350° oven 1 hour. Serves 4.

Swedish Meatballs

1½ pounds ground meat	1 teaspoon salt
½ cup bread crumbs	½ teaspoon pepper
½ cup milk	¼ teaspoon nutmeg
1 egg	1 can (11 oz.) mushroom
1 finely chopped onion	sauce
1 chopped garlic clove	2 tablespoons cooking oil

Mix all ingredients and shape into 1 inch balls. Brown slowly in oil. Drain. Add mushroom sauce and simmer 20 minutes. Serves 6.

Tamale Casserole

1 pound ground meat	soup
1 can (28½ oz.) tamales	1 teaspoon salt
1 can (8¾ oz.) whole-	¼ teaspoon pepper
kernel corn	¼ cup grated Parmesan
1 large, chopped onion	cheese
1 can (10¾ oz.) tomato	

Brown meat and remove. Sauté onion in drippings. Alternate layers of tamales, meat, corn, onion, salt, and pepper. Cover with tomato soup thinned with a little water. Sprinkle top with grated cheese. Bake in 350° oven

30 minutes. Serves 4.

Tamale Pie

1 pound ground meat	1 teaspoon salt
1 chopped onion	¼ teaspoon pepper
1 chopped garlic clove	1 can (29 oz.) tomatoes
2 teaspoons chili powder	1 package corn chips

Brown meat and remove. Sauté onion and garlic in drippings. Drain. Mix meat, onion, garlic, tomatoes, and seasonings. Alternate layers of corn chips and meat mixture in casserole. Bake in 350° oven 30 minutes. Serves 4.

Tacos

1 pound ground meat	10 corn tortillas
1 tablespoon onion flakes	½ cup cooking oil
½ teaspoon garlic salt	Chopped lettuce and
2 cans (4 oz. each)	tomatoes
taco sauce	

Slowly brown meat and drain. Add onion flakes, garlic, and 1 can taco sauce. Slightly steam tortillas. Place 1 tablespoon of filling on each tortilla. Fold in half and fasten with a toothpick. Brown in hot oil and remove toothpick. Open just enough to add salad.

To make fluffy tacos, proceed in same manner except dip filled tortilla in thin batter before frying.

Serve with the second can of taco sauce. Serves 4-6.

Texas Chili

1½ pounds ground meat	2-3 tablespoons chili
2 tablespoons shortening	powder
½ cup chopped onion	2 teaspoons salt
1 chopped garlic clove	3 cups water
1 teaspoon cumin seed	1 can (16 oz.) tomatoes

Brown meat in shortening. Add onion and garlic and cook until onion is limp. Drain. Add cumin seed, chili powder, salt, tomatoes, and water. Cover and simmer 1 hour. Thicken with flour mixed with a little water. Serve with pinto beans. Serves 4-6.

Western Loaf

1½ pounds ground meat	½ teaspoon chili powder
1 diced onion	1 teaspoon salt
1 minced garlic clove	½ teaspoon pepper
1 tablespoon chopped parsley	½ cup cooked rice
	2 eggs
2 tablespoons chopped chives	½ cup catsup
	Bread crumbs

Mix all ingredients, except bread crumbs. Place in greased loaf pan. Sprinkle with crumbs. Bake in 350° oven 1 hour. Serve with tomato or mushroom sauce. Serves 6.

Sauces
and
Stuffings

Sauces

There are many new sauces, canned, packaged, and bottled that are very good with wild game and fowl. Sauces should compliment not dominate the meat. Homemade sauces should be cooked over low heat. Combine the liquid and flour carefully to avoid lumps. Use a hand beater to dissolve lumps. If butter-based sauces separate, add a small amount of cold water.

Allemande Sauce

Very good with leftover pheasant, quail, or turkey.

2 tablespoons flour	1 teaspoon lemon juice
2 tablespoons butter	2 tablespoons cream
1 cup broth	Salt and pepper to taste
1 egg yolk	

Melt butter over low heat and stir in flour. Remove from heat. Stir in salt, pepper, slightly beaten egg yolk, lemon juice, and cream. Beat well. Makes 1½ cups.

Béarnaise Sauce

2 tablespoons chopped onion	3 slightly beaten egg yolks
1 tablespoon chopped green pepper	⅓ cup butter
½ cup wine vinegar	½ teaspoon salt
1 tablespoon butter	¼ teaspoon pepper
	¼ teaspoon nutmeg

Simmer the onion, pepper, and vinegar 10 minutes. Strain. Discard onion and pepper. Cool. Beat in egg yolks and the 1 tablespoon butter. Cook very slowly in double boiler, about 4 minutes. Remove from heat. Stir in the rest of the butter, salt, pepper, and nutmeg. Continue heating and stirring until thick. Serve immediately. Makes ¾ cup.

Mushroom Sauce

2 tablespoons butter
2 tablespoons flour
1 can (10½ oz.) beef
  bouillon
1 teaspoon Worcester-

shire sauce
1 can (4 oz.) sliced
  mushrooms
Salt and pepper to taste

Melt butter over low flame and add flour slowly. Stir until well blended. Add bouillon and Worcestershire sauce. Simmer, stirring constantly until thick. Add mushrooms and more water if necessary. Makes 1½ cups.

Béchamel Sauce

2 tablespoons flour
2 tablespoons butter
1 can chicken consommé

3 tablespoons cream or
  canned milk
Salt and pepper to taste

Melt butter in double boiler and stir in flour. Add consommé and stir until mixture is thickened. Add cream. Makes 1½ cups.

Velouté Sauce

¼ cup butter
¼ cup flour
2 cups chicken broth

½ teaspoon salt
¼ teaspoon pepper
¼ teaspoon nutmeg

Melt butter over low heat. Add flour and blend well. Remove from heat. Gradually stir in broth. Cook slowly stirring constantly until thick and smooth. Add seasonings. Makes 2 cups.

Wine Sauce

This is excellent served over liver and ham.

2 tablespoons butter
2 tablespoons flour
1 chicken bouillon cube

1 cup boiling water
¼ cup sherry wine
½ teaspoon sugar

Melt butter over low heat. Add flour and stir.

Remove from heat. Dissolve bouillon cube in boiling water. Add to flour mixture. Cook slowly stirring constantly until thickened. Remove from heat. Stir in wine and sugar. Simmer about 3 minutes. Makes 1 cup.

Orange Sauce for Game

3 tablespoons butter
¼ cup flour
1½ cups stock
Pinch salt
½ teaspoon grated

orange rind
⅓ cup orange juice
1 tablespoon sherry
Dash Tabasco sauce

Melt the butter. Stir in flour. Add the stock slowly stirring constantly. Add salt. Keep in double boiler over hot water. Before serving, stir in orange juice, rind, sherry, and Tabasco. Excellent with wild duck or goose. Makes 2 cups.

Cherry Sauce

After ducks, geese, or game have been removed from roasting pan, add 3 tablespoons kirsch, 1 can (10¾ oz.) or packet of beef gravy, and 1 cup sour cherries. Simmer about 5 minutes. Season and serve over duck or game.

Cumberland Sauce

½ cup currant jelly
  (or any tart jelly)
1 tablespoon vinegar
½ teaspoon Dijon
  mustard

¼ cup sherry wine
½ teaspoon grated
  lemon rind
Dash Tabasco sauce

Break up the jelly. Stir in rest of the ingredients. If too strong add a little water. Makes ¾ cup.

Herb Sauce

2 tablespoons butter
1 cup currant (or tart)
  jelly

Pinch each rosemary,
  thyme, and savory

Melt butter over low heat. Stir in jelly and herbs. Heat for a few minutes. Good with game, duck, or goose. Makes 1 cup.

Barbecue Sauce

2 tablespoons butter	1 teaspoon dry mustard
2 tablespoons chopped onion	1½ teaspoons sugar
1 minced garlic clove	¼ cup Worcestershire sauce
1 cup wine vinegar	1½ cups catsup
½ cup water	Juice of ½ lemon

Melt butter. Sauté onions and garlic slowly until limp but not brown. Add remaining ingredients and cook slowly until thickened. Makes 2½ cups.

Creole Sauce

3 tablespoons oil	1 teaspoon chili powder
½ cup chopped green pepper	1 tablespoon sugar
½ cup chopped onion	1 bay leaf
1 chopped garlic clove	1 tablespoon dried celery leaves
1 can (20 oz.) tomatoes	Salt and pepper to taste

Heat oil in skillet. Add onion, green pepper, and garlic. Simmer until soft (about 5 minutes). Add remaining ingredients and simmer about 30 minutes. Makes 2 cups.

Tomato Sauce

1 can (29 oz.) tomatoes	1 tablespoon sugar
½ cup chopped onion	3 whole cloves
1 bay leaf	½ teaspoon mustard
½ teaspoon salt	3 tablespoons butter
¼ teaspoon pepper	3 tablespoons flour

Mix tomatoes, onion, mustard, and spices together in a saucepan. Simmer 20 minutes. Strain through a sieve, or mix in blender. Melt the butter in the saucepan. Stir in flour and mix. Slowly add the seasoned tomato juice. Cook and stir constantly 5 minutes or until thickened. Makes 2 cups.

Mustard Sauce

Very good with cold sliced tongue, or other cold meats. Mix ½ cup mayonnaise with 1 teaspoon Worcestershire sauce and 1 teaspoon Dijon mustard. Makes ½ cup.

Pickled Green Chili Sauce

½ cup sugar	green chili or 5 small
½ cup vinegar	cans chopped chili
1 teaspoon salt	1 teaspoon celery seed
2½ cups fresh, roasted,	1 teaspoon mustard seed
peeled, and chopped	2 minced garlic cloves

Mix sugar, vinegar, salt, celery seed, and mustard seed. Simmer 10-15 minutes or until it makes a light syrup. Add chili and garlic to syrup (do not cook). Place in jars and refrigerate. Makes 2½ cups for 2 jars.

Green Chili Sauce

Mix 1 peeled, chopped tomato, 1 small, chopped onion, 1 can (4 oz.) chopped green chili, 1 teaspoon lemon juice, and salt and pepper to taste. Makes 1 cup.

Horseradish Sauce

½ cup sour cream	horseradish
(or substitute)	1 teaspoon lemon juice
3-4 tablespoons	¼ teaspoon salt

Mix all ingredients. If too thick add a small amount of milk. This is especially good with cold sliced antelope, deer, or elk served on hot rye bread. Makes ¾ cup.

Hot Sauce

1 tablespoon vinegar	1 teaspoon Dijon (hot)
2-3 tablespoons grated	mustard
horseradish	½ cup mayonnaise

½ teaspoon salt
Dash cayenne pepper

1 can (4 oz.) chopped
green chili

Mix all ingredients. Makes 1 cup.

Stuffings

These stuffings were meant to accommodate birds weighing 3-5 pounds.

Bread Stuffing

2 cups bread crumbs
½ cup broth
¼ cup melted butter
1 beaten egg

½ teaspoon salt
¼ cup chopped onion
½ cup chopped celery
1 teaspoon savory

Mix broth, melted butter, egg, and seasonings. Fluff with bread crumbs. Toss in onion and celery. Mix lightly. Stuff bird loosely.

Brown Bread Stuffing

2 tablespoons oil
2 tablespoons chopped
   onion
½ cup chopped celery
½ teaspoon salt
¼ teaspoon garlic
   powder
¼ teaspoon pepper

½ teaspoon sage
1 tablespoon chopped
   parsley
¼ cup stock or milk
¼ cup melted butter
2 cups brown bread
   crumbs or crumbled
   toast

Brown the onion in oil. Add the stock or milk and melted butter. Add the seasonings and toss with bread crumbs. Add the celery and mix lightly. Stuff bird loosely.

Cornbread Stuffing

1 beaten egg

¼ cup diced celery

3 tablespoons chopped onion	butter
½ cup stock	½ teaspoon sage
2 cups crumbled cornbread	½ teaspoon salt
3 tablespoons melted	¼ teaspoon pepper
	½ teaspoon garlic salt

Mix beaten egg with stock and melted butter. Add seasonings. Toss lightly with the cornbread. Stuff bird loosely.

Chestnut Stuffing

1 quart chestnuts	1 teaspoon salt
¼ cup bread crumbs	¼ teaspoon pepper
½ cup melted butter	½ teaspoon savory
1 tablespoon onion juice	

Shell and blanch chestnuts. Cook in boiling water until tender. Rub through coarse sieve. Mix lightly with the rest of the ingredients. Stuff bird loosely.

Fruit Stuffing

2 cups bread crumbs	½ cup chopped apple
2 tablespoons melted butter	½ cup chopped, dried apricots
¼ cup water	¼ cup chopped pecans
¼ cup red wine	½ teaspoon nutmeg
1 teaspoon salt	

Toss together bread crumbs and butter. Add apple, apricots, and pecans. Sprinkle with salt and nutmeg. Moisten with water and wine. Let stand 30 minutes before stuffing the bird.

Mushroom Stuffing

3 cups bread crumbs	1 teaspoon salt
½ cup melted butter	1 teaspoon chopped parsley
1 can (8 oz.) chopped mushrooms and liquid	½ teaspoon thyme

Mix butter with mushroom liquid. Add mushrooms and seasonings. Toss lightly with bread crumbs. Stuff bird loosely.

Potato Stuffing

2 cups hot mashed
  potatoes
1 cup bread crumbs
½ teaspoon salt
¼ teaspoon pepper

2 teaspoons onion juice
4 tablespoons melted
  butter
1 teaspoon sage

Mix mashed potatoes with seasonings. Toss with bread crumbs. Pour melted butter over mixture and mix lightly.

Raisin-nut Stuffing

2 cups bread crumbs
⅓ cup melted butter
½ cup chopped, seedless
  raisins
½ cup chopped walnut

meats
1 teaspoon salt
¼ teaspoon pepper
½ teaspoon sage

Mix together crumbs, raisins, and nuts. Add seasonings. Pour over melted butter and toss lightly.

Rice Stuffing

1 cup bread crumbs
1 chopped onion
4 cups boiled rice
1 cup broth

½ teaspoon sage
½ teaspoon thyme
½ teaspoon salt
¼ teaspoon pepper

Mix bread crumbs, onion, and rice with seasonings. Moisten with broth and toss lightly.

Wild Rice and Mushroom Stuffing

⅓ cup chopped onion

¼ cup butter

**1 can (8 oz.) chopped
mushrooms and liquid
3 cups boiled wild rice**

**1 teaspoon salt
¼ teaspoon pepper**

Brown onion slowly in butter. Stir in mushrooms, liquid, wild rice, salt, and pepper. Toss lightly.

Glossary

a la king: food, such as fowl and bland meats, served in a rich cream or white sauce.

a la mode: braised beef with vegetables. Also refers to pie or cake topped with ice cream.

au gratin: food mixed with cream or white sauce, covered with bread crumbs and cheese, and baked until browned.

au jus: meat served in its natural juices.

baste: to moisten with liquid while cooking to prevent drying and to add flavor.

blanch: to plunge into boiling water to lighten or facilitate in peeling.

blanquette: a fricassee or stew made with a white sauce.

bouillon: a clear broth usually made from beef. Also made by dissolving commercially prepared bouillon cubes in hot water.

braise: to brown meat or other foods on all sides in a small amount of hot fat. Add liquid, cover, and simmer.

broth: liquid in which meat, poultry, or vegetables have been cooked.

canapé: a thin piece of bread, toast, etc., spread or topped with cheese, caviar, anchovies, or other foods.

chutney: a sauce or relish of East Indian origin containing both sweet and sour ingredients, with spices and other seasonings.

condiments: sauces or relishes accompanying food, such as catsup, Worcestershire sauce, or prepared mustard. They are usually served with a main dish.

consommé: a clear, strong soup made by boiling meat and bones slowly and for a long time in order to extract their nutritive properties.

crêpes: a thin, light, delicate pancake, served with filling and sauce as a main dish or dessert.

croutons: small bread cubes sautéed or toasted in the oven.

cube: to cut into ½-inch cubes.

devil: to prepare with hot seasoning, such as mustard or hot sauce.

dice: to cut into very small pieces or cubes.

dredge: to cover or coat, usually with flour, seasoned mixture, or sugar.

drippings: fats and juices that come from meat as it cooks.

filet mignon: an individual steak cut from the tenderloin of beef.

fork tender: meat or vegetables cooked until a fork can be inserted with ease.

garlic clove: one section from the whole garlic bulb.

giblets: the heart, liver, gizzard, and neck of a fowl, often cooked separately.

goulash: the Hungarian term for stew, usually a heavy stew.

kirsch: cherry liqueur, mainly produced in Switzerland.

marinade: an acid (tomato or lemon juice) or a mixture of oil and acid (French dressing), in which food is soaked to develop flavor and tenderness.

marinate: to let foods stand in a marinade before cooking or serving.

mince: to chop very fine.

parboil: to partially cook in water or other liquid, before baking or frying.

pâté: a smooth, richly seasoned mixture usually made from chicken livers.

pâté de foie gras: a smooth, richly seasoned mixture made from goose liver.

pressure cook: to cook quickly or to preserve foods by means of superheated steam under pressure.

prosciutto: spiced ham, often smoked, that has been cured by drying; always sliced paper-thin for serving.

ragout: a thick, well-seasoned French stew made with meat, vegetables, and spices.

ramekins: small, individual, ovenproof casserole dishes.

render: to melt the fat from fatty meats.

rissole: a nicely seasoned meat mixture, wrapped in rich pastry and fried in deep fat.

roux: a cooked mixture of butter and flour, used to thicken soups and sauces.

sauté: to cook in a skillet on top of the range in a little butter or other shortening.

sauerbraten: a pot roast of beef, marinated in a mixture of vinegar, sugar, and seasonings.

score: to cut narrow gashes, part way through fat, in meats before cooking.

simmer: to cook below boiling point on top of range.

skewer: to thread pieces of food on a long wooden or metal pin for broiling or grilling so they will hold their shape while cooking.

spätzle: very similar to noodles and served with meat as a main dish.

spit cook: to cook food on a revolving spit (rotisserie).

stew: to cook food in liquid slowly over a long period of time.

stock: richly flavored liquid in which meats or vegetables have been cooked.

stroganoff: meat browned with onion and cooked in a

sauce of sour cream, seasonings, and usually mushrooms.

suet: the hard fatty tissue about the loins and kidneys of meat processed to yield tallow.

tripe: stomach tissue of beef or lamb.

truss: to tie any meat, game, or poultry so that it will hold its shape while roasting.

tureen: a large, deep, covered dish for serving soup, stew, or other foods.

velouté: a basic, rich, white cream sauce.

vermicelli: a kind of pasta in the form of long, slender, solid threads, resembling spaghetti but thinner.

vinaigrette: a sauce made with vinegar or a combination of oil, vinegar, and seasonings.

Index